A Systematic and Integrative Model for Mental Health Assessment and Treatment Planning

A Systematic and Integrative Model for Mental Health Assessment and Treatment Planning

Julie Gosselin
Mélanie Joanisse

MOMENTUM PRESS
HEALTH

First published in 2017 by
Momentum Press®, LLC
222 East 46th Street, New York, NY 10017
www.momentumpress.net

ISBN-13: 978-1-94474-931-6 (print)
ISBN-13: 978-1-94474-932-3 (e-book)

Momentum Press Developing a Competency Based Mental Health Practice Collection

Cover and interior design by S4Carlisle Publishing Services Private Ltd., Chennai, India

First edition: 2017

10 9 8 7 6 5 4 3 2 1

Printed in the United States of America

Dedication

Mélanie Joanisse: I would like to dedicate this book to my clinical supervisors of the University of Ottawa (especially Dr. Marlene Best and my coauthor Dr. Gosselin), because their expertise and teachings influenced the development of our integrative framework. I wish to also dedicate this to my clinical students because their judicious questions and comments highlighted the importance of developing a coherent framework and ultimately made me a better clinician. At last, I would like to thank my husband, Norm, for his unconditional support.

Julie Gosselin: I would like to dedicate this book to my clinical students who, over the past decade, have taught me to refine my clinical thinking and to better articulate my clinical training observations. I want to especially thank my coauthor Dr. Mélanie Joanisse for agreeing to take on this challenge with me: your intellectual rigor and clinical acumen are at the core of the creation of this model. Finally, I would like to thank my husband and my family for their unwavering support.

Abstract

This book sets the stage by providing a clear, systematic, and integrative model for mental health assessment and treatment planning that can be used in a variety of clinical settings, with a diverse adult clinical population. This book advocates for the importance of considering all aspects of evidence-based practice (i.e., best available research, clinician's expertise, and experience, as well as clients' preferences and idiosyncrasies) when conducting assessments and delivering psychological treatments. Special attention is also given to the interdisciplinary aspects of delivering mental health care in today's fast-paced environments. If you are a seasoned clinician or a beginner therapist, you will surely find this book useful because it provides a general map that can be used regardless of your specific theoretical orientations. The applied nature of the content makes it easy and valuable for readers who wish to apply psychology integration to their own practice. Specifically, case vignettes have been developed to help readers gain a better understanding on how to apply the integrative interprofessional framework into their practice. Finally, professors and supervisors will also find this book worthwhile as the authors incorporated a chapter on the supervision and evaluation of assessment and treatment planning competencies.

Keywords

assessment, evidence-based, integration, psychology, treatment

Contents

Acknowledgments ....*xi*

Chapter 1 A Transtheoretical Model for Psychotherapy
           Integration 1
Chapter 2 A Model of Assessment and Treatment Planning
           Fit for the Modern Clinician 19
Chapter 3 An Integrative Interprofessional Model for
           Psychological Assessment 31
Chapter 4 Conducting Psychological Assessment and Creating
           a Case Formulation 45
Chapter 5 An Integrative Interprofessional Model for
           Psychological Treatment Planning and
           Monitoring 61
Chapter 6 Treatment Delivery and Monitoring............................85
Chapter 7 Conducting an Intake and Treatment
           Planning Session 95
Chapter 8 The Supervision and Evaluation of Assessment
           and Treatment Planning Competency
           Development 113

Appendix A *121*
About the Authors...*137*
Index *139*

Acknowledgments

We would like to acknowledge Sheila N. Garland, PhD. Registered Clinical Psychologist and Assistant Professor of Psychology and Oncology at Memorial University, St. John's, Newfoundland for her judicious comments on the initial version of this book.

CHAPTER 1

A Transtheoretical Model for Psychotherapy Integration

For many years, practitioners and researchers have attempted to find the Holy Grail of psychotherapy—the particular treatment approach that could lead to the best treatment outcomes for clients. Although this quest was noble, it led to the development of approximately 500 "brands" of psychotherapy (Pearsall, 2011) and what we would call an "outbreak of initialisms" (eg., CBT, EFT, DBT, REBT, MBSR, MBCT, EMDR, IPT, AEDP, and ACT to name a few). Witnessing this proliferation of psychotherapies over the past decades has become quite overwhelming for students in graduate schools and experienced therapists alike. How are we supposed to learn and master all of these approaches? If a therapist is only knowledgeable in one or two of these approaches, is this therapist less competent than his or her peers? One simple answer to these questions could have been: select the therapy that is the most efficacious, and you will be fine. However, it is not that simple. To date, outcomes studies comparing the effectiveness of various psychotherapies have not found one approach to be superior to others (Luborsky, Singer, & Luborsky, 1975; Wampold et al., 1997 or see Wampold, 2001 for a review). Luborsky et al. (1975) concluded in favor of Dodo-bird-verdict: "Everyone has won, and all must have prizes" (Luborsky et al., 1975, p. 1003) initially advanced by Rosenzweig (1936). Although some have contested this view or warned against its simplistic interpretation (Crits-Christoph, 1997; Howard, Krause, Saunders, & Kopta, 1997; Stiles, Shapiro, & Elliott, 1986), these findings show the need for clinicians to be able to take a step back from their "practice as usual" and deliberately reflect on: what works, for whom, by whom, and in what context. This chapter gives a brief overview of the main difficulties and problems with the research and practice of psychotherapy that prompted the "rise of integration" (Norcross, 2005, p. 7)[1] and highlight the need to develop a coherent and flexible framework to help clinicians assess and treat clients as well as monitor their outcomes in today's complex and fast-paced environment, *regardless* of their theoretical orientation. In this era of evidence-based practice (EBP), we believe integrative treatment planning is not incongruent with this movement and can actually offer great insights and an organized framework for the complexities of modern care service delivery.

EBP from Medicine to Psychology

EBP originated in the medical field. Sackett, Rosenberg, Gray, Haynes, and Richardson (1996) defined EBP medicine as:

> The conscientious, explicit, and judicious use of current best evidence in making decisions about the care of individual patients. The practice of evidence based medicine means integrating individual clinical expertise with the best available external clinical evidence from systematic research. (p. 71)

In later years, the definition was refined by emphasizing patient-related variables, such as the patient's values and preferences (Institute of Medicine, 2001; Sackett, Straus, Richardson, Rosenberg, & Haynes, 2000) actions, circumstances, and clinical state (Haynes, Devereaux, & Guyatt, 2002; Straus, Glasziou, Richardson, & Haynes, 2011). The aim is to integrate each of these components to optimize patient management. EBP was implemented in other disciplines, such as nursing, physiotherapy, and pharmacy. In line with the zeitgeist, the American Psychological Association (APA) 2005 Presidential Task Force on EBP comprising scientists and practitioners reviewed the literature and reflected on how to best define evidence-based practice in psychology (EBPP). From these deliberations emerged the following definition: "Evidence-based practice

---

[1] See Norcross (2005) for a more in-depth discussion and presentation on these factors in Nocross and Goldfried (2005)'s Handbook of psychotherapy integration; a must read for anyone wishing to better understand psychotherapy integration.

in psychology is the integration of the best available research with clinical expertise in the context of patient characteristics, culture and preference" (American Psychological Association, 2006, p. 273). Therefore, EBP emerges from the interplay of research, clinician, and patient-centered variables.

Misconceptions of EBP

Unfortunately, EBP has been sometimes misunderstood as the utilization of manualized treatment protocols that have been empirically validated, often using a randomized clinical trial (RCT). For some, the utilization of the treatment manual is not conceived as one part of the treatment delivery as it should be, but it becomes the whole treatment. The clinician's delivery of the treatment, the client idiosyncrasies, and the interaction between these variables are not considered as important. This is problematic for various reasons, and the full discussion is outside of the scope of this book,[2] but we wish to address the main issues with this approach: (1) clinicians often do not treat a homogeneous sample of patients with a single diagnosis; (2) good therapy is inherently responsive to client needs and preferences; and (3) RCTs cannot adequately address all issues related to psychological health.

However, we are not against the use of validated treatment manuals or treatment based on diagnosis, nor do we reject RCTs; we believe them to be laudable. In some instances, it can make pragmatic sense to use a *DSM-5* diagnosis to orient treatment plan given how the broader health care system is organized. RCTs can also be pertinent in addressing some scientific endeavors and has greatly helped increase the legitimacy of psychological treatment in the health care system where pharmaceutical approaches were often seen as the treatment of choice (see Barlow, 2004 for a review). What we denounce is the systematic, rigid use of these manuals and calling it "evidence-based practice" or the use of *DSM-5* disorders as analogous to a comprehensive case formulation. Instead, through our discussion of the three aforementioned

---

[2]We encourage you to read Norcross, Beutler, and Levant (2006) for relevant and interesting debates on EBP.

issues, we wish to make a case for a balanced approach and consideration of all components of EBP and are in favor of multiple sources of evidence to inform practice.

Problem 1: Diagnosis as Case Formulation

In some graduate schools, it has been the norm to assess a person to formulate a diagnosis and then plan treatment according to this diagnosis. The logic seems bulletproof and fairly congruent with our experience when going to a physician's office. "The doctor says I have X then I will be prescribed Y." Yet, research has depicted a more complex picture when applied to psychotherapy, and when this diagnosis–treatment logic is applied to real life, problems quickly emerge. If the case conceptualization is only informed by the diagnosis, what happens if a client presents with polysymptomatology? In community settings, the patient population often presents with comorbid psychological and physical disorders. Complexity and variability are customary, not the exception. Therefore, to provide the best treatment, where should the clinician start? What variables should be considered and prioritized? Is the low-socioeconomic-status Caucasian male patient suffering from chronic obstructive pulmonary disease, chronic pain, depression, and generalized anxiety to be treated with the same psychological treatment as the high-income African American woman with chronic pain, persistent depressive disorder, and anxiety not otherwise specified?

Some researchers and clinicians have argued in favor of diagnostic-dependent treatments (see Chambless et al., 1996, 1998). Probably the most prolific approach in this area has been cognitive behavioural therapy (CBT) that has provided a plethora of disorder-specific treatment protocols (see Beck, Rush, Shaw, & Emery, 1979; Leahy & Holland, 2000). Unfortunately, research has not supported this linear view (Miller, Duncan, & Hubble, 2005; Wampold, 2010). First, the same disorder seems to be treatable by a wide range of approaches. For example, depression and posttraumatic stress disorder can be effectively treated with various intended-to-be therapeutic treatments (see Wampold, 2010 for a discussion). Second, the same treatment can be efficacious for more than one disorder. An illustration of this has been unified treatment protocols (or transdiagnostic treatment) that emphasize the commonalities versus the differences between some disorders. Unified treatment plans focusing on the underlying common elements of anxiety and depression have shown some promising results (see McEvoy, Nathan, & Norton, 2009 or Reinholt & Krogh, 2014 for a review). The idea that for a specific diagnosis one main approach should be used seems incredulous in light of Lambert and Barley's (2001; see also Asay & Lambert, 1999) estimation that specific techniques only account for 15% of the explained variance in psychotherapy outcome. In fact, they suggest that approximately 40% of the variance in treatment outcomes is explained by factors that occur outside of the therapy context (e.g., events in the patient's life and level of social support), emphasizing the importance of considering the broader context when developing a treatment plan as opposed to treating only a specific disorder.

In sum, we strongly believe that the therapist should consider the patient as a whole, not just a list of symptoms that match a particular diagnosis. As Westen (2006a) pointed out "if patients came in neat packages, so could treatments. But everything we know suggests that they do not" (p. 397). Case formulation should therefore be comprehensive and consider variables related to the patient, which will permit the tailoring of his or her care (e.g., stage of change, coping style, or treatment expectations).

Problem 2: EBP as Synonymous to Manualized Evidence-Based Treatment Plans

Responsiveness has been defined as "behavior being influenced by emerging context" (Kramer & Stiles, 2015, p. 277). Applied to psychotherapy, this means that clinicians react and adapt to their clients and vice versa. EBP needs to make room for the fluidity of the clinician–patient interaction or relationship and the context in which it arises (Stiles, 2006; Stiles, Honos-Webb, & Surko, 1998; Greenberg & Watson, 2006). It cannot be the rigid application of a treatment manual; flexibility seems to be key. Using a psychodynamic treatment plan, Owen and Hilsenroth (2014) showed a significant positive association between a clinician's level of flexibility over time when delivering treatment to a given patient and treatment outcomes. Research on treatment adherence[3] (or the integrity of treatment delivery) has produced divergent results, with some showing a positive association between adherence and outcome (for example see Hogue et al., 2008) and others showing no significant associations between adherence and symptom change (Boswell et al., 2013; Webb, DeRubeis, & Barber, 2010). This could highlight that the relationship between adherence and outcome is more complex. In line with this view, Huppert, Barlow, Gorman, Shear, & Woods (2006) found preliminary results suggesting an interaction between the client's motivation and adherence to a CBT protocol of panic disorder when predicting outcomes. Specifically, their results showed that for patients who were rated as motivated by their therapist, treatment adherence did not significantly relate to change in panic severity. In contrast, patients rated as having low motivation for treatment achieved better results with therapists displaying lower levels of adherence. Interestingly, adherence seems inconsequential when a good therapeutic relationship is present. Barber et al. (2006) found that the contribution of adherence to treatment outcomes in drug counselling was nullified when therapist and clients had a strong therapeutic alliance. In contrast, moderate treatment adherence was linked to better outcomes when the strength of the therapeutic alliance was weaker, lending support to the statement that: "therapists who do therapy by the book develop better relationships with their manuals than with clients" (Duncan, & Miller, 2006, p. 145.). Taken together, these results seem to suggest that although adherence can be important to produce significant change, it should not trump responsiveness or eclipse the context in which this relationship materializes. Again, this seems to support the need to consider the interaction of all variables included in the EBP model.

Problem 3: EBP as Synonymous to a Specific Empirically Supported Treatment (EST) Validated with an RCT

Another misconception of EBP seems to stem from the sophism that one particular approach is the piece de resistance, especially when it has

---

[3]For a more comprehensive discussion on treatment adherence see Wampold and Imel (2015).

been validated using RCTs. According to Tucker and Roth (2006), there seems to be this "hierarchical views that favor randomized controlled trials (RCTs) over other forms of evidence" (p. 101) to answer important research questions (e.g., causal inferences) or inform of treatment efficacy. Janicek (2003, as cited in Tucker & Reed, 2008) refers to five levels to classify evidence related to treatment efficacy: level 1 (RCTs), level 2 (nonrandomized trials), level 3 (analytical observational studies), level 4 (multiple times series, place comparisons, "natural" experiments), and level 5 (expert opinions, case series or reports, descriptive occurrence). It is clear that RCTs can produce valuable information and should not be discarded (Hollon, 2006), but EBP cannot be reduced to the application of research produced by RCTs and should include other source of evidence. Several authors have argued in favor of "evidentiary pluralism" for EBP especially when applied to psychology (see Tucker & Roth, 2006; Tucker & Reed, 2008) because some questions might be better investigated using other methodologies, such as case studies (Stiles, 2006b) or process research studies (Greenberg & Watson, 2006). By focusing on efficacy (superior or not) and neglecting variables related to the process of change, RCTs do not help investigate "what" pertaining to the theoretical model helped achieve symptom change (Greenberg & Watson, 2006). Furthermore, more research is needed to determine if the results from RCTs can be "transported" to real-life contexts with more heterogeneous samples of clinicians and patients (Westen, 2006b). This seems especially important for the usefulness of ESTs with ethnic minority groups, given the scarcity of RCTs with this population (Sue & Zane, 2006).

The supremacy of RCTs is not only unfortunate for the advancement of knowledge and treatment development but also for the publicly funded treatments available to patients. As Reed (2006) noted, "medical researchers and health care policy makers view the purpose of RCTs as providing a basis for health policy" (p. 17). In order to become an EST, the APA's Division 12 (Clinical Psychology) established criteria (see *Task Force on Promotion and Dissemination of Psychological Procedures*, 1993). To be deemed "well-established," the efficacy of the treatment must have been demonstrated by "at least two good between group design experiments" or "a large series of single case design experiments (n>9) demonstrating efficacy" (Chambless et al., 1998, p. 4). Criteria also include the use of a treatment manual, clearly defined sample, and effects demonstrated by a minimum of two investigators or teams (Chambless et al., 1998). Although rigorous, some have argued that these criteria are biased and favor therapeutic modalities that lend themselves more easily to RCTs, which has resulted in greater representations of cognitive and behavioural approaches in APA'S ESTs lists (*Task Force on Promotion and Dissemination of Psychological Procedures*, 1995) and by extension to publicly funded programs (see Castelnuovo, 2010 for a discussion).

Specifically, in the United States and elsewhere (e.g., United Kingdom, Sweden, and Australia), major initiatives have been allocated funds (often billions of dollars) to promote dissemination and access to evidence-based psychological treatments (see McHugh & Barlow, 2010). This idea seemed promising and long overdue. However, these initiatives tend to focus on a specific approach to deliver. Most often the recommended treatments are CBT. Although positive outcomes for some of these programs have been published, such as the UK's Improving Access to Psychological Therapies (IAPT) program (see Fonagy & Clark, 2015; Gyani, Shafran, Layard, & Clark, 2013), the implementation and outcomes of these programs have been controversial. Some have indicated that these efforts might not have been as fruitful as initially expected. For example, to ensure higher rates of recovery and ultimately increase the return to work rates, the Swedish Government and the Swedish Association of Local Authorities and Regions founded a program, Rehabilitation Guarantee, aimed at helping individuals living with mild and moderate levels of mental illness access specific treatments (mainly CBT). A recent report by the Swedish National Audit Office (2015) reveals that the program was largely ineffective. The main reasons cited were the lack of qualified assessments to access treatment needs and preferences, and the emphasis on the modality/method of treatment as opposed to the intended outcome (i.e., successful work reintegration). Similarly, in his editorial on the IAPT program, Timimi (2015) denounced how this initiative mainly aimed at increasing access to CBT treatments might be costlier than comparable mental health services already available pre-IAPT without providing superior outcomes.

The reason for these mixed results is most likely complex. One could argue that the implementation of these programs was not optimal and lacked fidelity. In their review of current efforts to disseminate and implement evidence-based psychological treatment, McHugh and Barlow (2010) warned against the rushed implementation of these programs without consensus on best practice guidelines to optimize success (for example, level of competence of the provider, and assessment and monitoring of training procedures).

Conversely, it can be reasoned that the focus on particular modalities, in contrast to programs that give patients a voice (i.e., that consider their preference and particular needs) and options on which psychological treatment they would like to undertake (or other treatments) could be another factor that lead to these outcomes. Recent results showing fairly equivalent results between CBT, person-centered, and psychodynamic treatments in a primary care setting seems to lend support to a broader array of options to patients (Stiles, Barkham, Mellor-Clark, & Connell, 2008). And even more interesting, in their update of the IAPT, Fonagy and Clark (2015) report that in the past 2 years, more employment and training efforts have been allocated to non-CBT modalities compared to CBT. Supporting Wampold and Imel's (2015, March) claim that it would be "unwise to mandate any particular treatment" when implementing broad-range programs.

By discussing these issues, we hope you can develop a better understanding of EBP to inform your own practice. EBP should be a guide to enhance decision making in a collaborative fashion between the therapist and the client. It should not be synonymous with a specific modality. All components of EBP should be integrated to better serve your clients.

EBP and Integration

Given the proliferation of therapies, the demonstrated usefulness of multiple treatment plans and modalities, the complexity of the clinical picture of clients and the environment they live in, and the need to be responsive therapists, it is not surprising that therapists have started to "integrate" almost intuitively. When reviewing profiles of therapists online, the trend is showing: "I am a primarily cognitive-behavioral-based therapist but I add some elements of interpersonal psychotherapy," "I am an experiential therapist with training in mindfulness-based therapies." Interestingly, we seem to be describing our professional identities like we describe our

Zodiac Signs: "I am a Libra and my ascendant is Scorpio"! Such a desire to integrate seems understandable but also can appear a bit disorganized.

Also, when observing the "new" treatment protocols and the enthusiasm by which some clinicians are selling their "new brand of psychotherapy" that will surely save us all, one cannot help but feel a certain déjà-vu or dare we say "integration." New cognitive behavioral treatment plans are not being called emotion-focused CBT. Motivational interviewing incorporates a lot of patient-centered psychotherapy components. Some principles of mindfulness psychotherapy oddly resemble Eugene Gendlin's focusing (Gendlin, 1996). This is not to criticize the development of these approaches but to highlight that their apparent novelty is more a reflection of their integrative nature than actual original ideas.

At the same time, some researchers have steered away from the dogma of the single approach and focused their energy on "What Works" in psychotherapy. Of importance is the commons factors movement that started early but seemed to have attracted more attention with the work of Norcross and colleagues. Norcross (2005) notes that the common factors approach "seeks to determine the core ingredients that different therapies share in common, with the eventual goal of creating more parsimonious and efficacious treatments based on their commonalities" (p. 9). Furthermore, Prochaska and Diclemente's (1984 as cited in Prochaska, 1995) transtheoretical model of behavioral change has also helped support the need to tailor our work to a client's particular stage of change and has promoted the idea that different modalities can be useful at different points and times within the therapeutic process. Change-process researchers have also informed us on what works for whom and when, further demystifying what leads to good outcomes (see for example, Greenberg & Pinsof, 1986; Greenberg & Watson, 2006; Honos-Webb, Stiles, Greenberg, & Goldman, 1998). In addition, the outcome monitoring movement has directed our attention to the need to routinely assess the impact of our interventions and monitor progress. This seems especially important given the fact that clinicians are often poor judges of treatment outcome and tend to overestimate its success (see Lambert, 2013; Walfish, McAlister, O'Donnell, & Lambert, 2012) and that patients' feedback can improve outcomes, especially when deterioration is occurring (Lambert, Harmon, Slade, Whipple, & Hawkins, 2005). Since then, various measures and outcome management systems have been developed (Outcome Questionnaire 45; Lambert et al., 2004; Clinical Outcomes in Routine Evaluation, Core System Group, 1998; the Partners for Change Outcome Management System, Miller & Duncan, 2000; 2004) that are not dependent on the nature of the psychological treatment being offered. In a field where resources (both human and financial) are often limited, it is crucial that clinicians be accountable to their client and third-party payers.

Putting It All Together: The Integrative Model

The main issues discussed in this chapter reveal the need for a good case formulation model that permits clinical sensitivity, a model that includes core ingredients being known to lead to change and permits flexibility to consider the client's preferences, characteristics, and culture. This model should also be in constant evolution to incorporate new research findings and should emphasize the need to monitor treatment outcomes. Lastly, this model should take into account the need to evaluate competence in delivering such a model (versus the competence in delivering a particular treatment approach). This model should be able to guide assessment, treatment planning, treatment delivery as well as evaluation (treatment outcome and therapeutic competence). As you embark on this discovery of psychotherapy integration, we wish to offer some food for thoughts and encourage you to deliberate on your own EBPP. Hopefully, you will find our integrative model useful in this journey.

References

American Psychological Association. (2006). Evidence-based practice in psychology. *American Psychologist, 61*(4), 271–285. doi:10.1037/0003-066X.61.4.271.

Asay, T. P., & Lambert, M. J. (1999). The empirical case for the common factors in therapy: Quantitative findings. In M. A. Hubble, B. L. Duncan, & S. D. Miller (Eds.), *The heart and soul of change: What works in therapy* (pp. 23–55). Washington, DC: American Psychological Association Press. doi:10.1037/11132-001.

Barber, J. P., Gallop, R., Crits-Christoph, P., Frank, A., Thase, M. E., Weiss, R. D., et al. (2006). The role of therapist adherence, therapist competence, and alliance in predicting outcome of individual drug counseling: Results from the National Institute Drug Abuse Collaborative Cocaine Treatment Study. *Psychotherapy Research, 16*(2), 229–240. doi:10.1080/10503300500288951.

Barlow, D. H. (2004). Psychological treatments. *American Psychologist, 59*(9), 869–878. doi:10.1037/0003-066X.59.9.869

Beck, A. T., Rush, J. A., Shaw, B. F., & Emery, G. (1979). *Cognitive therapy for depression*. New York, NY: Guilford Press.

Boswell, J. F., Gallagher, M. W., Sauer-Zavala, S. E., Bullis, J., Gorman, J. M., Shear, M. K., et al. (2013). Patient characteristics and variability in adherence and competence in cognitive-behavioral therapy for panic disorder. *Journal of Consulting and Clinical Psychology, 81*(3), 443–454. doi:10.1037/a0031437.

Castelnuovo, G. (2010). Empirically supported treatments in psychotherapy: Towards an evidence-based or evidence-biased psychology in clinical settings? *Frontiers in Psychology, 27*(1), 1–10. doi:10.3389/fpsyg.2010.00027.

Chambless, D. L., Baker, M. J., Baucom, D. H., Beutler, L. E., Calhoun, K. S., Crits-Cristoph, P., et al. (1998). Update on empirically validated therapies, II. *The Clinical Psychologist, 51*(1), 3–16.

Chambless, D. L., Sanderson, W. C., Shoham, V., Bennett Johnson, S., Pope, K. S., Crits-Cristoph, P., et al. (1996). An update on empirically validated therapies. *The Clinical Psychologist, 49*(2), 5–18.

Crits-Christoph, P. (1997). Limitations of the dodo bird verdict and the role of clinical trials in psychotherapy research: Comment on Wampold et al. (1997). *Psychological Bulletin, 122*(3), 216–220. doi:10.1037/0033-2909.122.3.216.

Core System Group. (1998). *Core system information management handbook*. Leeds, UK: Core System Group.

Duncan, B. L., & Miller, S. D. (2006). Does manualization improve therapy outcomes: Treatment manuals do not improve outcome. In J. C. Norcross, L. E Beutler, & R. F. Levant (Eds.), *Evidence-based practices in mental health: Debate and dialogue on the fundamental questions* (pp. 140–149). Washington, DC: American Psychological Association Press.

Fonagy, P., & Clark, D. M. (2015). Update on the Improving Access to Psychological Therapies programme in England: Commentary on … Children and Young People's Improving Access to Psychological Therapies. *BJPsych Bulletin, 39*(5), 248–251. doi:10.1192/pb.bp.115.052282.

Gendlin, E. T. (1996). *Focusing-oriented psychotherapy: A manual of the experiential method.* New York, NY: Guilford Press.

Greenberg, L., & Pinsof, W. M. (1986). *The Psychotherapeutic process: A research handbook.* New York, NY: Guilford Press.

Greenberg, L. S., & Watson, J. C. (2006). What qualifies as research on which to judge effective practice? Change process research. In J. C. Norcross, L. E Beutler, & R. F. Levant (Eds.), *Evidence-based practices in mental health: Debate and dialogue on the fundamental questions* (pp. 81–89). Washington, DC: American Psychological Association Press.

Gyani, A., Shafran, R., Layard, R., & Clark, D. M. (2013). Enhancing recovery rates: Lessons from year one of IAPT. *Behaviour Research and Therapy, 51*(9), 597–606. doi:10.1016/j.brat.2013.06.004.

Haynes, R. B., Devereaux, P. J., & Guyatt, G. H. (2002). Clinical expertise in the era of evidence-based medicine and patient choice. *Evidence Based Medicine, 7,* 36–38.

Hogue, A., Henderson, C. E., Dauber, S., Barajas, P. C., Fried, A., & Liddle, H. A. (2008). Treatment adherence, competence, and outcome in Individual and family therapy for adolescent behaviour problems. *Journal of Consulting and Clinical Psychology, 76*(4), 544–555. doi:10.1037/0022-006X.76.4.544.

Hollon, S. D. (2006). What qualifies as research on which to judge effective practice? Randomized control trials. In J. C. Norcross, L. E. Beutler, & R. F. Levant (Eds.), *Evidence-based practices in mental health: Debate and dialogue on the fundamental questions* (pp. 96–105). Washington, DC: American Psychological Association Press.

Honos-Webb, L., Stiles, W., Greenberg, L., & Goldman, R. (1998). Assimilation analysis of process-experiential psychotherapy: A comparison of two cases. *Psychotherapy Research, 8*(3), 264–286. doi:10.1080/10503309812331332387.

Howard, K. I., Krause, M. S., Saunders, S. M., & Kopta, S. M. (1997). Trials and tribulations in the meta-analysis of treatment differences:

Comment on Wampold et al. (1997). *Psychological Bulletin, 122*(3), 221–225. doi:10.1037/0033-2909.122.3.221.

Huppert, J. D., Barlow, D. H., Gorman, J. M., Shear, M. K., & Woods, S. W. (2006). The Interaction of motivation and therapist adherence predicts outcome in cognitive behavioral therapy for panic disorder: Preliminary findings. *Cognitive and Behavioral Practice, 13*(3), 198–204.

Institute of Medicine. (2001). *Crossing the quality chasm: A new health system for the 21st century.* Washington, DC: National Academies Press.

Kramer, U., & Stiles, W. B. (2015). The responsiveness problem in psychotherapy: A review of proposed solutions. *Clinical Psychology: Science and Practice, 22*(3), 277–295. doi:10.1111/cpsp.12107.

Lambert, M. J. (2013). Outcome in psychotherapy: The past and important advances. *Psychotherapy, 50*(1), 42–51. doi:10.1037/a0030682.

Lambert, M. J., & Barley, D. E. (2001). Research summary on the therapeutic relationship and psychotherapy outcome. *Psychotherapy: Theory, Research, Practice, Training, 38*(4), 357–361. doi:10.1037/0033-3204.38.4.357.

Lambert, M. J., Harmon, C., Slade, K., Whipple, J. L., & Hawkins, E. J. (2005). Providing feedback to psychotherapists on their patients' progress: Clinical results and practice suggestions. *Journal of Clinical Psychology, 61*(2), 165–174. doi:10.1002/jclp.20113.

Lambert, M. J., Morton, J. J., Hatfield, D., Harmon, C., Hamilton, S., Reid, R. C., et al. (2004). *Administration and scoring manual for the OQ-45.* Orem, UT: American Professional Credentialing Services.

Leahy, R.L., & Holland, S. J. (2000). *Treatment plans and interventions for depression and anxiety.* New York, NY: The Guildford Press.

Luborsky, L., Singer, B., & Luborsky, L. (1975). Comparative studies of psychotherapies: Is it true that "everyone has won and all must have prizes?" *Archives of General Psychiatry, 32*(8), 995–1008. doi:10.1001/archpsyc.1975.01760260059004.

McEvoy, P. M., Nathan, P., & Norton, P. J. (2009). Efficacy of transdiagnostic treatments: A review of published outcome studies and future research directions. *Journal of Cognitive Psychotherapy, 23*(1), 27–40.

McHugh, R. K., & Barlow, D. H. (2010). The dissemination and implementation of evidence-based psychological treatments. *American Psychologist, 65*(2), 73–84. doi:10.1037/a0018121.

Miller, S. D., & Duncan, B. L. (2000, 2004). *The outcome and session rating scales: Administration and scoring manual.* Chicago, IL: ISTC.

Miller, S. D., Duncan, B. L., & Hubble, M. A. (2005). Outcome-informed clinical work. In J. C. Norcross, & M. R. Goldfried (Eds.), *Handbook of psychotherapy integration* (2nd ed., pp. 84–104). New York, NY: Oxford University Press.

Norcross, J. C. (2005). A primer on psychotherapy integration. In J. C. Norcross, & M. R. Goldfried (Eds.), *Handbook of psychotherapy integration* (2nd ed., pp. 3–23). New York, NY: Oxford University Press.

Norcross, J. C., Beutler, L. E., & Levant, R. F. (Eds.). (2006). *Evidence-based practices in mental health: Debate and dialogue on the fundamental questions.* Washington, DC: American Psychological Association Press.

Norcross, J. C., & Goldfried, M. R. (Eds.). (2005). *Handbook of psychotherapy integration,* (2nd ed.). New York, NY: Oxford University Press.

Owen, J., & Hilsenroth, M. J. (2014). Treatment adherence: The importance of therapist flexibility in relation to therapy outcomes. *Journal of Counseling Psychology, 61*(2), 280–288. doi:10.1037/a0035753.

Pearsall, P. (2011). *500 therapies: Discovering a science for everyday living.* New York, NY: Norton.

Prochaska, J. O. (1995). An eclectic and integrative approach: Transtheoretical therapy. In A. S. Gurman, & S. B. Messer (Eds.), *Essential psychotherapies: Theory and practice* (pp. 403–440). New York, NY: Guilford Press.

Reed, G. M. (2006). What qualifies as evidence of effective practice? Clinical expertise. In J. C. Norcross, L. E. Beutler, & R. F. Levant (Eds.), *Evidence-based practices in mental health: Debate and dialogue on the fundamental questions* (pp. 13–23). Washington, DC: American Psychological Association Press.

Reinholt, N., & Krogh, J. (2014). Efficacy of tansdiagnostic cognitive behaviour therapy for anxiety disorders: A systematic review and meta-analysis of published outcome Studies. *Cognitive Behaviour Therapy, 43*(3), 171–184.

Rosenzweig, S. (1936). Some implicit common factors in diverse methods of psychotherapy. *American Journal of Orthopsychiatry, 6*(3), 412–415. Retrieved from http://search.proquest.com/docview/1492509392?accountid=14701.

Sackett, D. L., Rosenberg, W. M., Gray, J. A., Haynes, R. B., & Richardson, W. S. (1996). Evidence based medicine: What it is and what it isn't. *BMJ: British Medical Journal, 312*(7023), 71–72.

Sackett, D. L., Straus, S. E., Richardson, W. S., Rosenberg, W., & Haynes, R. B. (2000). *Evidence based medicine: How to practice and teach EBM* (2nd ed.). London, UK: Churchill Livingstone.

Stiles, W. B. (2006a). What qualifies as research on which to judge effective practice? Dialogue: Convergence and contention. In J. C. Norcross, L. E Beutler, & R. F. Levant (Eds.), *Evidence-based practices in mental health* (pp. 105–110). Washington, DC: American Psychological Association Press.

Stiles, W. B. (2006b). What qualifies as research on which to judge effective practice? Case studies. In J. C. Norcross, L. E. Beutler, & R. F. Levant (Eds.), *Evidence-based practices in mental health: Debate and dialogue on the fundamental questions*, (pp. 57–64). Washington, DC: American Psychological Association Press.

Stiles, W. B., Barkham, M., Mellor-Clark, J., & Connell, J. (2008). Effectiveness of cognitive-behavioural, person-centred, and psychodynamic therapies in UK primary-care routine practice: Replication in a larger sample. *Psychological Medicine, 38*(5), 677–688. doi:10.1017/S0033291707001511.

Stiles, W., Honos-Webb, L., & Surko, M. (1998). Responsiveness in psychotherapy. *Clinical Psychology: Science and Practice, 5*(4), 439–458.

Stiles, W. B., Shapiro, D. A., & Elliott, R.. (1986). Are all psychotherapies equivalent?. *American Psychologist, 41*(2), 165–180. doi:10.1037/0003-066X.41.2.165.

Straus, S. E., Glasziou, P., Richardson, W. S., & Haynes, R. B. (2011). *Evidence-based medicine: How to practice and teach EBM* (4th ed.). New York, NY: Churchill Livingstone.

Sue, S. S., & Zane, N. (2006). How well do both evidence-based practices and treatment as usual satisfactorily address the various dimensions of diversity? Ethnic minority populations have been neglected by evidence-based practices. In J. C. Norcross, L. E. Beutler, & R. F. Levant (Eds.), *Evidence-based practices in mental health: Debate and dialogue on the fundamental questions*, (pp. 329–337). Washington, DC: American Psychological Association Press.

Swedish National Audit Office. (2005). Summary: The rehabilitation guarantee is not working-rethink or discontinue. (Report number: RIR 2015:19). Retrieved from http://www.riksrevisionen.se/Page-Files/23011/Summary_2015_19.pdf.

Task Force on Promotion and Dissemination of Psychological Procedures. (1993). American Psychological Association, Division 12. Retrieved from http://www.div12.org/sites/default/files/InitialReportOfThe-ChamblessTaskForce.pdf.

Task Force on Promotion and Dissemination of Psychological Procedures. (1995). Training in and dissemination of empirically validated treatments: Report and recommendations. *The Clinical Psychologist, 48*(1), 3–23.

Timimi, S. (2015). Update on the Improving Access to Psychological Therapies programme in England: Author's reply. *BJPsych Bulletin, 39*(5), 252–253. doi:10.1192/pb.bp.115.052399.

Tucker, J. A., & Reed, G. M. (2008). Evidentiary pluralism as a strategy for research and evidence-based practice in rehabilitation Psychology. *Rehabilitation Psychology, 53*(3), 279–293. doi:10.1037/a0012963.

Tucker, J. A., & Roth, D. L. (2006). Extending the evidence hierarchy to enhance evidence-based practice for substance use disorders. *Addiction, 101*(7), 918–932. doi:10.1111/j.1360-0443.2006.01396.x.

Walfish, S., McAlister, B., O'Donnell, P., & Lambert, M. J. (2012). An investigation of self-assessment bias in mental health providers. *Psychological Reports, 110*(2), 639–644. doi:10.2466/02.07.17. PR0.110.2.639- 644.

Wampold, B. E., Mondin, G. W., Moody, M., Stich, F., Benson, K., Ahn, H., et al. (1997). A meta-analysis of outcome studies comparing bona fide psychotherapies: Empirically, "All must have prizes". *Psychological Bulletin, 122*(3), 203–215. doi:10.1037/0033-2909.122.3.203.

Wampold, B. E. (2001). *The great psychotherapy debate: Models, methods, and findings*. Mahwah, NJ: Lawrence Erlbaum Associates.

Wampold, B. E. (2010). The research evidence for the common factors models: A historically situated perspective. In B. L. Duncan, S. D. Miller, B. E. Wampold, & M. A. Hubble (Eds.), *The heart and soul of change: Delivering what works in therapy* (2nd ed., pp. 49–81). Washington, DC: American Psychological Association Press.

Wampold, B. E., & Imel, Z. E. (2015). *The great psychotherapy debate: The evidence for what makes psychotherapy work* (2nd ed.). New York, NY: Taylor & Francis Inc.

Wampold, B. E., & Imel, Z. E. (2015). What do we know about psychotherapy?—and what is there left to debate? Retrieved from http://www .societyforpsychotherapy.org/what-do-we-know-about-psychotherapy-and-what-is-there-left-to-debate.

Webb, C. A., DeRubeis, R. J., & Barber, J. P. (2010). Therapist adherence/competence and treatment outcome: A meta-analytic review. *Journal of Consulting and Clinical Psychology, 78*(2), 200–211. doi:10.1037 /a0018912.

Westen, D. I. (2006a). Are efficacious laboratory-validated treatments readily transportable to clinical practice ? Dialogue: Convergence and contention. In J. C. Norcross, L. E. Beutler, & R. F. Levant (Eds.), *Evidence-based practices in mental health: Debate and dialogue on the fundamental questions* (pp. 395–397). Washington, DC: American Psychological Association Press.

Westen, D. I. (2006b). Are efficacious laboratory-validated treatments readily transportable to clinical practice? Transporting laboratory-validated treatments to the community will not necessarily produce better outcomes. In J. C. Norcross, L. E. Beutler, & R. F. Levant (Eds.), *Evidence-based practices in mental health: Debate and dialogue on the fundamental questions,* (pp. 383–393). Washington, DC: American Psychological Association Press.

CHAPTER 2

A Model of Assessment and Treatment Planning Fit for the Modern Clinician

Over the past 40 years, the field of clinical psychology has been in constant evolution, with some suggesting that the half-life of any knowledge in clinical psychology is approximately 5 years, or about the amount of time a regular clinical psychology graduate student will take to complete his /her graduate professional training. As such, its main challenge has been to provide training programs with the very best, up-to-date information to train future professionals, while recognizing the crucial importance of ongoing professional development for all clinical psychology professionals. In the first chapter, we learned about the inherent challenges to adopting an evidence-based approach to case formulation, treatment planning and delivery, and how various integrative models of care have informed the evolution of treatment approaches.

At the same time, we recognize that professional psychology has begun to adopt a competency-based approach to training and evaluation within its graduate programs. A competency is a complex behavior that encompasses the ongoing development of an integrated set of knowledge, skills, attitudes, and judgments enabling one to effectively perform the activities required in a given occupation or function to the standards expected in knowing how to be in various and complex environments and situations (McNair, 2005). A competency framework can help students and practitioners to make sense of the learning process, differentiate topics by relevance, and apply learning to practical situations. Anchored in competency benchmarks (Fouad et al., 2009), this approach focuses on objective, observable behaviors that have been identified as salient to the demonstration of particular professional competencies. As such, it can be a valuable tool to orient training objectives, as well as performance feedback. Assessment represents one of the competency domains identified in these benchmarks, which are interacting grouping of activities that comprise part of a whole. It defines this area as the "assessment and diagnosis or problems, capabilities and issues with individuals, groups, and /or organizations" (Fouad et al., 2009, p. S16). It includes as its essential components to determine readiness for entry to practice the capacity to: (1) independently select and implement multiple methods and means of evaluation in ways that are responsive to and respectful of diverse individuals, couples, families, and groups; (2) independently understand the strengths and limitations of diagnostic approaches and interpretation of results from multiple measures for diagnosis and treatment planning; (3) independently select and administer a variety of assessment tools and integrate results to accurately evaluate a presenting question appropriate to the practice site and to the broader area of practice; (4) use case formulation and diagnosis for intervention planning in the context of stages of human development and diversity; (5) independently and accurately conceptualize the multiple dimensions of the case based on the results of assessment; and (6) communicate results in written and verbal form clearly, constructively, and accurately in a conceptually appropriate manner. Behavioral anchors further help to operationalize each competency criteria.

In 2013, Hatcher and colleagues published a revised version of the benchmarks, which included assessment competency in what has now been defined as the first of three "functional competencies," with evidence-based practice, intervention, and consultation (p. 86). However, while these benchmarks are helpful in clearly defining "what" needs to be taught to develop competency in assessment and treatment planning, the "how" remains somewhat unclear to both trainees and trainers. The authors of the revised benchmarks (Hatcher et al., 2013) acknowledged this fact in stating the crucial need for practical applications of the comprehensive competency benchmarks for training in professional psychology. This is where evidence-based training comes into play.

In their article presenting core principles for training in evidence-based psychology, Beck and colleagues (2014) argue that clinical practice must be based on research. In presenting their framework for the training of graduate students, the first key principle of evidence-based doctoral training highlights the integration of assessment and treatment, and the fostering of a data-based practice. In the context of an evidence-based and person-centred approach to assessment, the authors state that assessment and treatment are "tightly integrated" (Beck et al., 2014, p. 413), with assessment guiding clinical decisions about case formulation, diagnosis, and treatment conceptualization. In addition, students should be taught to consider assessment of an ongoing process that continues throughout the treatment, so that the clinician is able to make data-based decisions about modifying or terminating treatment. Information pertaining to client preferences, including economic resources, diversity issues, level of impairment, and perceived quality of life should all be considered. This suggests a high level of integration, where both conceptual and empirical information must be taken into consideration for optimal efficacy. But what is integration?

Between a quarter to a third of North American psychologists identify themselves as eclectic or integrative, which means that the integrative approach would be the most prevalent theoretical orientation among practitioners (Norcross, 2011). That being said, the manner in which this integration occurs in practice can take a number of forms (Norcross and Halgin, 2005). First, some clinicians work mostly within one theoretical orientation but discriminate between those patients who can benefit from their approach and those who would likely benefit more from a different approach. The latter are referred systematically to clinicians offering these other treatments. We will call this integrative model "differential referral." Integration happens here through the development of a network of mental health professionals who can work together to refer particular patients to the most appropriate practitioner within their network. A second form of integration is called "technical eclecticism." Here the clinician focuses his/her attention to selecting the best technique and/or intervention, from different theoretical models, based on the particular problems faced by his/her patient. Therefore, integration occurs at the technical level rather than at a conceptual or theoretical level. In fact, "theoretical integration" is a third form of integration where the clinician integrates two or more theoretical models together to create his/her own theoretical approach that can be applied from case formulation to treatment planning. An alternative form of this type of integration is called "integrative assimilation," which represents a more tentative synthesis of different models of practice. In this fourth form, the clinician usually begins by adopting one theoretical model of practice and, over time, integrates additional perspectives and practices from other approaches to expand his /her scope of practice. Finally, a "common factors" approach represents an integration of core concepts common to different models in order to create a more efficacious and parsimonious model of practice.

Evidence points toward the need for modern psychological practice to use an integrative approach. The new context of practice is one marked by an increasing speed at which services must be delivered, as well as an increase in the complexity of presenting patient symptoms. Treatment protocols by diagnostic profile, although useful, do not fully appreciate the impact of the interconnection between various factors of influence that can complicate or mitigate any particular clinical presentation. In addition, patients presenting with psychological problems often are also coping with a variety of physical problems that must be taken into consideration in both case formulation and treatment delivery. Finally, most clinicians are restricted in their practice by a limited allowed number of sessions per patient, which also highlights the important role of prioritization in treatment planning. As such, the modern clinician must have a powerful map that is flexible and adaptive, while remaining robustly anchored in evidence-based care. This cannot be accomplished without a certain level of integration according to Paris (2013), who notes that the division of psychological work into theoretical schools is a mark of an immature science.

Integration does not preclude specificity, just like common factors may be necessary but not always sufficient to realize effective care. In fact, recent meta-analytic findings (Norcross and Wampold, 2011) indicate that the quality of the therapeutic relationship as well as common factors have developed a strong evidence base for their therapeutic effectiveness, independent of the specific type of treatment. Therefore, it would seem that the modern clinician requires an integrative model that capitalizes on common factors of therapeutic change, while taking into consideration particular individual, cultural, and socioeconomic factors that may involve the inclusion of specific interventions that have shown efficacy in addressing these particular patient-specific concerns.

One such integrative model developed for assessment and treatment planning comes from internal medicine and is called "evidence-based medicine" (Youngstrom, Choukas-Bradley, Calhoun, and Jensen-Doss, 2015). This model was developed as a philosophy and a set of skills that can help manage complex information so that clinicians can rely on data-based practices to improve client care. Youngstrom and colleagues (2015) admit that this model was developed almost entirely independently from clinical psychology, although it could stand to offer a useful framework for the practice of psychological assessment and treatment planning. The model involves twelve steps: (1) identifying the most common diagnoses in the practice setting, (2) benchmarking base rates, (3) evaluating risks and moderators for most common diagnoses, (4) synthesizing intake instruments into revised probabilities, (5) interpreting cross-informant data patterns, (6) adding narrow and incremental assessments to clarify diagnosis, (7) adding necessary intensive methods to finalize diagnosis and case formulation, (8) finish assessment for treatment planning and goal setting, (9) measure treatment processes (ongoing treatment monitoring), (10) chart progress and outcome, (11) monitor maintenance and relapse warnings, and (12) seek and use client preferences (Youngstrom et al., 2015, p. 24).

Although interesting for its focus on research-based and data-based decision-making, "evidence-based medicine" is firmly anchored into a medical model of clinical psychology where the main goal of a psychological assessment remains diagnosis. Recent meta-analytical findings in clinical psychology (Norcross and Wampold, 2011) indicate that efforts to promote evidence-based care without including the therapeutic relationship are "seriously incomplete and potentially misleading" (p. 98), while patient-centred care must include tailoring treatment planning to specific patient characteristics in addition to diagnosis to enhance the effectiveness of treatment. Given this, the "evidence-based medicine" model seems like a good starting point in developing an integrative framework for psychological assessment and treatment planning, but additional development is still necessary to fully meet the practical and professional needs of the modern mental health clinician.

Indeed, well-researched, clearly defined, and measurable competencies are becoming the norm across a number of health professions. These efforts have also resulted in a growing interest for the development of interprofessional competencies necessary for the provision of effective evidence-based care in the context of interprofessional collaboration. Interprofessional collaboration has been defined as "the process of developing and maintaining effective interprofessional working relationships with learners, practitioners, patients/clients/families and communities to enable optimal health outcomes" (Canadian Interprofessional Health Collaborative, 2010, p. 8). In Canada, where the authors of this book both practice as clinical psychologists, this role has been spearheaded by the Canadian Interprofessional Health Collaborative (CIHC), which is made up of health organizations, health educators, researchers, health professionals, and students from across Canada. Their mission is to improve interprofessional education and collaborative patient-centred practice as key elements to developing and maintaining effective health care teams and ensuring quality patient outcomes. In 2010, CIHC released a National Interprofessional Competency Framework to respond to the need of identifying a set of interprofessional competencies that can be tested and either verified, adjusted, or discarded. Interprofessional competencies describe the complex integration of knowledge, skills, attitudes, and judgments that allow a health provider to apply their professional expertise effectively into all collaborative situations. This "living" document was developed by a working group of volunteers from a number of health professions. They identified a total of six competency domains required for effective interprofessional collaboration. These include: (1) interprofessional communication, (2) patient/client/family/community-centred care, (3) role clarification, (4) team functioning, (5) collaborative leadership, and (6) interprofessional conflict resolution. The framework posits that the application of these six competency domains is interdependent of each other, where the two first sets of competencies act as support to the integrated whole of the latter four. In addition, the framework recognizes the role of contextual issues, complexity of presenting symptoms, and quality improvement as factors of influence on interprofessional collaboration.

Therefore, we began by discussing the advent of competency benchmarks in clinical psychology and its impact on the training of future mental health professionals. We also discussed the need for assessment and treatment planning practices to be grounded in research, or what has been called using an evidence-based approach. Given the empirical evidence for the need to adapt our professional practices to patient characteristics, assessment and treatment planning practices should also include a patient-centred approach. We presented the steps involved in the evidence-based model of medicine and discussed its applicability to clinical psychology. We also described how integration was necessary as part of an evidence-based, patient-centred, competency-based approach to assessment and treatment planning. Finally, we explored the parallel development of interprofessional competency domains, resulting in the National Interprofessional Competency Framework in Canada (CIHC, 2010). This latter framework also presents with a high level of integration that includes an evidence-based, patient-centred approach to interprofessional collaboration.

We strongly believe that these form the necessary ingredients to an effective framework for modern mental health clinicians to use as part of their assessment and treatment planning work. First, assessment and treatment planning practices must be anchored in the demonstration of competency behaviors (e.g., competency benchmarks). Second, diagnostic and treatment planning decisions should be based on empirical and research evidence, which requires an evidence-based and patient-centred approach that is both rigorous and flexible, and which views the assessment process as ongoing even after treatment as begun (thus including the use of treatment monitoring tools). Third, interprofessional collaboration has become more important in modern mental health care systems and must be taken into consideration to provide optimal patient outcomes. Fourth, the most effective and parsimonious approach to deliver such care as part of professional mental health assessment and treatment planning practices is to create an integrative framework that can guide the mental health clinician in organizing available information to competently inform key clinical decisions.

The last consideration that must be addressed as part of this integrative framework is the need to anchor the development of competencies in assessment and treatment planning within the overall development of two related competency domains: (1) professionalism and (2) reflective practice. Fouad and colleagues (2009) defined professionalism as "professional values and ethics as evidenced in behavior and comportment that reflects the values and ethics of psychology, integrity, and responsibility" (p. S9). It also included attention to accountability and concern for the welfare of others, as well as the necessity to develop a professional identity. This conceptualization of professionalism is similar to many others that tend to focus on aspirational values, professional codes, professional norms, and/or professional regulations.

However, Bilodeau (2015) suggests that professionalism should not simply be reduced to these different lists of items. Instead, his own definition aims to orient professional development and reflective practice as part of a more general and all-encompassing process of professionalism. His definition hinges on the interaction between three main components. The first one is trust. Trust refers to the difference in power that exists between the professional and the user of his/her professional service. This difference is normally significant, because the user is in a vulnerable state, seeking answers about what he/she has been coping with, and presenting with various limits in knowledge or abilities to effectively address presenting symptoms in an autonomous manner. The user has to trust that the professional will understand what the problem is and, more importantly, have the competencies to help solve the problem or at least address it to the extent that it is possible to do so. Thus, trust is at the core of professionalism, binding the professional and the user together. The second component is the fiduciary relationship that links the professional and the user of the professional service. As a community or society, we have chosen to erect certain knowledge and abilities to a level that merits financial compensation for its execution. As such, professionalism is anchored in the context of a fiduciary relationship where the expectation is that the user will "get their money's worth." Professionalism implies that the professional will do their best to meet those expectations. Finally, the third component is compassion. It refers to the capacity of the professional to empathize with the user of the professional service in order to meet their needs in the best manner. It also includes related concepts of benevolence, nonmaleficence, and the respect for autonomy. In fact, compassion is implied by the trust that the user gives to the professional and their acceptance of the fiduciary relationship. No one wants to work with a professional care that is not compassionate, nor is anyone interested in paying for services that are untrustworthy. Therefore, we would argue that competent assessment and treatment planning must also be grounded in professionalism.

At the same time, competent assessment and treatment planning practices cannot occur without reflective practice. Fouad and colleagues (2009) define this competency as a "practice conducted with personal and professional self-awareness and reflection; with awareness of competencies; and with appropriate self-care" (p. S10). This is very important because evidence-based practice is rooted in the proactive self-assessment of what is known, what is needed to be known, and what is unknown in our field of work, as well as in the self-assessment of what the professional is able to do competently, what they are not able to do competently, and the planning of ongoing professional development to maintain and further develop current competencies. In addition, patient-centred care relies on the self-awareness of the professional and his/her ability to reflect on the impact of particular patient characteristics, as well as the impact of their own perspective about particular patient characteristics, on their ability to make effective data-based clinical decisions for optimal patient outcomes. Finally, the integration of various types of knowledge, attitudes, values, and judgments necessary for the competent practice of assessment and treatment planning requires a high level of capacity for self-reflection, in order to maintain professional rigor and compassionate flexibility to effectively address the complexity of patient symptoms. Reflective practice orients clinical judgment, which is the mental health professional's main tool of practice. Without clinical judgment, professional practice becomes rote, limited to technical know-how. In this context, self-care becomes paramount. Just like a chef who meticulously maintains his blades to provide perfect cuts of meat, or the soldier who meticulously maintains his rifle to ensure its optimal accuracy, or the athlete who meticulously maintains his body to ensure maximal performance, mental health professionals must meticulously maintain their clinical competencies through self-care so that their clinical judgment will remain sharp and well-supported by reflective practice anchored in integrative evidence-based, patient-centred knowledge, abilities, and values.

References

Beck, J. G., Castonguay, L. G., Chronis-Tuscano, A., Klonsky, E. D., McGinn, L. K., and Youngstrom, E. A. (2014). Principles for training in evidence-based psychology: Recommendations for the graduate curricula in Clinical Psychology. *Clinical Psychology: Science and Practice, 21*(4), 410–424.

Bilodeau, A. (2015). Union ou balkanisation: une voie pour un professionalisme commun. In J. Gosselin, P. S. Greenman, and M. Joanisse (Eds.), Le développement professionnel en soins de santé primaire au Canada : Nouveaux défis, Presses de l'Université du Québec, pp.1–15.

Canadian Interprofessional Health Collaborative. (2010). A National Interprofessional Competency Framework, 36 pages. Retrieved from http://www.cihc.ca/files/CIHC_IPCompetencies_Feb1210.pdf.

Fouad, N. A., Grus, C. L., Hatcher, R. L, Kaslow, N. J., Hutchings, P. S., Madson, M. B., et al. (2009). Competency benchmarks: a model for understanding and measuring competence in professional psychology across training levels. *Training and Education in Professional Psychology, 3*(4-Suppl), S5–S26.

Hatcher, R. L., Fouad, N. A., Grus, C. L., Campbell, L. F., McCutcheon, S. R., and Leahy, K. L. (2013). Competency benchmarks: Practical steps toward a culture of competence. *Training and Education in Professional Psychology, 7*(2), 84–91.

McNair, R. P. (2005). The case for educating health care students in professionalism as the core content of interprofessional education. *Medical Education, 39*, 456–464.

Norcross, J. C. (2011). *Psychotherapy relationships that work: Evidence-based responsiveness* (2nd ed.). London, UK: Oxford Press.

Norcross, J. C., and Halgin, R. P. (2005). Training in psychotherapy integration. In J. C. Norcross, M. R. Goldfried (Eds.), *Handbook of psychotherapy integration* (pp. 439–458). New York, NY: Oxford University Press.

Norcross, J. C., and Wampold, B. E. (2011). Evidence-based therapy relationships: Research conclusions and clinical practices. *Psychotherapy, 48*(1), 98–102.

Paris, J. (2013). How the history of psychotherapy interferes with integration. *Journal of Psychotherapy Integration, 23*(2), 99–106.

Youngstrom, E. A., Choukas-Bradley, S., Calhoun, C. D., and Jensen-Doss, A. (2015). Clinical guide to the evidence-based assessment approach to diagnosis and treatment. *Cognitive and Behavioral Practice, 22*(1), 20–35.

CHAPTER 3

An Integrative Interprofessional Model for Psychological Assessment

In Chapter 2, we learned about the competency movement and how it contributed to the development of competency-based training in professional psychology, as well as how integrative approaches fit within an evidence-based model of care. We also discussed the growing importance of interprofessional practice within health care, and the need to attend to both professionalism and reflective practice within early and ongoing professional development in psychological assessment and treatment planning. Now, after having anchored ourselves in both a better understanding of the challenges faces by modern professional psychologists as well as the main currents at the forefront of the development of best practices in professional training, we are ready to learn more about an evidence-based, integrative, and interprofessional model for psychological assessment.

The model presented in this chapter is based on both common factors and theoretical integration. It is designed to be useful to the majority of mental health professionals, regardless of their theoretical approach or the population they serve. As a result, this model can be used as a general framework for professional practice. In presenting our model, we assume that the clinician already possesses good basic clinical skills, both in terms of assessment and of treatment, and that he/she is familiar with at least one evidence-based model of care. For a detailed presentation of evidence-based models used in the assessment and treatment of mental disorders, we invite the reader to consult recent publications on this topic (Haynes, Smith, and Hunsley, 2011; Hunsley and Mash, 2008; Lambert, 2013, Nathan and Gorman, 2007).

To develop a useful model, its structure must take into consideration the key aspects that will help to create a clear map for the clinician. First, the model must take into consideration the complexity of the presenting problems. It must answer questions like: is this problem acute or chronic? Is this problem stemming from individual and/or systemic circumstances? Is there comorbidity among presenting issues? Second, the model must be able to identify the key factors that should be prioritized in the treatment plan, given available resources for treatment. As such, it must be grounded in the scientific literature and in empirical evidence, so that the clinician can mobilize the most appropriate resources toward exerting change in the client's life. In other words, the framework has to permit the identification of the key features most malleable to change using a minimum of financial, material, and human resources. This requires that the clinician be familiar with base rates of mental disorders in the population he/she serves, that he/she be familiar with the evidence base for relevant treatment modalities and approaches for the management and treatment of mental disorders, and that he/she understand and apply best practices in completing a differential diagnosis.

Third, the model must also be informed by a positive approach centered on client strengths. It has to be capable of capturing both problematic risk factors as well as protective factors that can promote resilience and facilitate/support positive change in the client's life. This would include previous coping strategies that have been used successfully by the client to manage this or other personal problems, available resources in the client's social circle and community that could be put to work to support the client's personal life changes, as well as potential resources that could be developed by the client with appropriate support.

Fourth, this model must pay special attention to the role of the circle of care and the interprofessional or interdisciplinary aspects of the case management so that the clinician can reflect on the relevance of including and collaborating proactively with other health professionals in treatment planning to optimize care. Finally, the model must also take into consideration prognostic concerns—that is, key client characteristics that could affect the success of the proposed treatment plan.

Our Model

The model we propose here is divided into six areas of inquiry. The first area is symptoms, and pertains to obtaining a detailed account of presenting concerns that could be the focus of treatment. The second area is personal history, and pertains to the client history as well as examining how this particular current problem fits into their own personal story. The third area is ecosystemic factors, and pertains to examining characteristics from the individual to the societal level that are exerting pressure (or helping to maintain resilience) in the client's life. The fourth area is interdisciplinary collaboration, and focuses on the potential inclusion of additional health professionals as part of an effective and strategic treatment plan. The fifth area is prognostic concerns, and delineates potential barriers to engaging fully in the treatment plan. Finally, the sixth area pertains to clinician-related and contextual variables that can affect both case formulation and treatment planning. We will now present each area in detail, as well as provide examples of questions that could be used to elicit relevant content from the client.

Symptoms

First, a detailed account of current and past symptomatology is necessary to gather evidence for diagnostic purposes. Inquiries should be made to establish the nature, severity, and duration of current mental health symptoms, including both precipitating and predisposing factors, what has been done to cope with them, and how successful these efforts have been, both currently and in the past (if applicable). Structured and semistructured interview protocols may be helpful in framing this line of questioning. We recommend that the reader familiarize him/herself with at least one of the following options: the Structured Clinical Interview for DSM-5 (SCID-5), the Interview Guide for Evaluating DSM-5 Psychiatric Disorders and the Mental Status Examination (Zimmerman, 2013), the Composite International Diagnostic Interview (CIDI), or the Mini International Neuropsychiatric Interview (MINI). In addition, it is important to establish what has prompted the person to seek out help at this particular time, and what may have contributed to the help-seeking behavior, including symptom worsening, lowered functioning in important areas of life, for example.

Example questions:
- What has prompted you to seek help now?
- Can you describe the problems you have been experiencing? Can you give me an example of what that is like for you from recent days?
- What have you done to cope with these issues? How successful were your efforts in managing these problems?
- How do you cope with stress generally?
- How have these symptoms affected your life? Has there been any adverse effects on important areas of your life, like work, school, or relationships?

Personal History

Next, it is important to recognize that the person is presenting at a particular moment in their own personal history, which carries implications for several aspects of their current presentation. Their age, their family of origin, and their social and professional experiences all represent facets of their life that could affect the manner in which the person perceives who they are now and the world around them. They present with their own worldview and beliefs about themselves and others that have been shaped by a plethora of events and encounters. The manner in which the person has learned to interact with those around him/her, and the manner in which he/she generally manages distress, will also be partially tributary to developmental variables. In addition, we must pay attention to potential premorbid health factors, both individual and familial, as well as the person's general health and well-being (both physical and psychological), and how these are related to their personal history. We strongly believe that an integrative assessment needs to consider not only the duration, frequency, and intensity of a particular problem but give weight to the developmental variables such as genetic predispositions, attachment history, individual and family history of psychiatric and physical illnesses, traumatic experiences, precipitating events, as well as resilience and risk factors that sculpted a person's life. Finally, clinicians must explore the client's own narrative and how they construct meaning when developing their case conceptualization instead of making assumptions about the impact of these experiences. What is the person's level of insight into how these problems developed over time? How do they interpret the role of past major crises into current difficulties? How have they coped with difficulties in the past and with what level of success? In addition, the clinician should pay attention to what the client has felt was useful or detrimental in helping them cope with their life struggles.

Example questions:
- Have you ever sought help before? How successful were you in addressing these (and possibly other) symptoms in the past?
- How long have you been coping with these symptoms? Has anything changed their nature or severity over time?
- Can you describe what was going on in your life when you first started to experience these symptoms?
- How do you make sense of what is happening in your life?

Ecosystemic Factors

Then, the clinician must assess the current issues from a biopsychosocial point of view, using an ecosystemic approach. This theory stipulates that an individual's experience depends largely on their environment. As such, to understand presenting issues, it is necessary to understand the individual in his/her singularity, and then within their family, and then within their community, and then within larger systems that may play a role in their unique experience. In this model, Brofenbrenner (1979) created a hierarchy placing the individual at the center of five levels of influence: first, the ontosystem (individual characteristics), second, the microsystem (the immediate life context in which the individual is experiencing his/her issues), third, the exosystem (the indirect effect of larger systems on the immediate systems in which the individual is embedded), fourth, the macrosystem (beliefs, values, culture, and politics espoused or imposed on the individual), and finally the chronosystem (the time in history and its associated characteristics that may play a role in the person's experience). In this context, the person is conceptualized as coping with a variety of mental and physical health conditions that exist within a particular socioeconomic and cultural context. For example, Lisa is a 26-year-old Latina woman with good capacity for resilience (ontosystem) and lives with her parents and her younger siblings while she completes a college degree to work in a daycare center (microsystems). She lives in subsidized housing and worries about being able to afford her own lodgings once she starts to work full-time because rent in the core of the city (where she intends to work) has increased significantly in recent years, and the alternative is to rent outside the city where the commute to work will make it difficult for her to see her family regularly (exosystem). Because she was brought up in a traditional and very religious household, she feels pressure to visit her family regularly or else she fears her family will feel abandoned by her (macrosystem). She is already stressed out by the fact that her parents disagree strongly with her choice to move out of their home before marriage, something she feels is appropriate since most of her female friends have done the same (chronosystem). As such, whether Lisa presents with depressive or anxious symptoms will inevitably be affected by these various levels of influence, and treatment planning should take into consideration these environmental pressures.

It is important to assess the life context of the person, the resources they have access to within their social network and their community, and the resources they have used in the past and those that may be available to them now. It is also important to note limitations and barriers imposed by particular socioeconomic and/or cultural characteristics that could impede the person's access to coping resources, or their full participation in the treatment offered. Finally, it is crucial to note potential diversity issues that may play a significant role in the delivery of services, especially those that relate to marginalization, acculturation, and victimization. Our goal is to better understand how the client's culture, worldview, and spirituality/religion, may influence presenting difficulties and response to treatment.

Example questions:
- Who can you turn to when you are feeling stressed?
- What values are most important to you?

- What are your priorities right now?
- How would you define yourself as a person?
- Can you tell me a bit about the important relationships in your life right now?
- What are the major stressors in your life right now?
- What kind of resources do you have available to help you cope with these issues? Are there any issues with accessing these when you need them?
- Are the resources available to you sufficient? Do you find them appropriate?

Interdisciplinary Collaboration

Once the previous areas have been investigated, it is useful to reflect on the potential need to broaden the scope of the recommendations that will be part of the treatment plan. We know that there is a reciprocal relationship between physical and psychological health, and that personal habits (e.g., sleep, nutrition, exercise, smoking, drinking, as well as risky sexual practices to name a few) and the capacity to take charge of these habits in a healthier and more sustainable manner are central to the management of many chronic health conditions, including many mental health disorders. As such, clinicians must be able to assess the potential role that these factors play in order to have a more comprehensive and holistic understanding of presenting concerns to optimize coordination of care. Mental health professionals can no longer afford to work in silos; they must learn to work together with other health professionals to maximize the effectiveness of their own treatment plan, as part of a larger plan to improve the client's overall health and well-being. To ensure a good flow of communication between all health providers involved, the clinician should discuss with the client who they would like to involve in their care and encourage interprofessional collaboration. Special attention should be given to treatment received in the past. For example, if a client has received treatment from a psychiatrist and psychologist while being an inpatient at a mental health clinic, it would be important for these professionals to collaborate with the providers delivering services in the community. Too often, this work is being done independently of other services offered, with the client having to repeat their history on several occasions and being confused about the role and contributions of each professional within their circle of care. Finally, it can be worthwhile to inquire about adherence of the client to the treatment plan recommended by other health professionals (for example, are they taking their medication as intended, are they having difficulty implementing or maintaining healthy life habits) and assess what are the barriers and facilitators to adherence that stem from either individual (for example, motivation, knowledge) or contextual (resources available) variables. This part of the assessment process can go as far as considering whether the person really needs a psychological treatment, or whether another type of treatment /provider (for example, kinesiologists or dietician) be more appropriate. This means that sometimes the clinician will need to take into consideration what is already in place to manage the client's concerns through other health services as part of their own treatment plan, and sometimes it means integrating the referral to other health professionals to increase the effectiveness of their own treatment recommendations, or recommending a referral to another service provider. The best way to accomplish this is to integrate it as part of the case formulation within the initial assessment process.

Example questions:
- What other health professionals are already involved in managing this person's presenting concerns? What is the client's qualitative experience in receiving these other services?
- Does the client feel confident that they can implement the recommendations made by other health professionals involved in their care (e.g., Will he/she follow through with recommended exercise/diet/medication regime)?
- What information should be communicated with the other health professionals involved in the circle of care in order to optimize treatment effectiveness?
- Would the client benefit from a referral to other health professionals as part of my recommendations?
- What are the potential barriers to including additional health professionals in the treatment plan, both from the client's

perspective (e.g., financial resources, client motivation), and from a contextual perspective (e.g., availability of such services in the community)?

Prognostic Considerations

This model also requires the integration of obtained information from all other surveyed areas to identify factors that could reasonably affect treatment recommendations and effectiveness. Here we include a number of variables identified by previous research, such as capacity of insight and self-reflection, client motivation toward engaging in treatment and toward various treatment options, rigid interpersonal dynamics or difficult personality traits, as well as symptom severity and chronicity (Anderson, 2006; Di Blasi, Harkness, Ernst, Georgiou, and Kleijnen, 2001; Nathan and Gorman, 2007; Norcross, 2011). Taken together, these different factors can help to orient treatment recommendations, such as what to prioritize early in treatment, who to involve within the circle of care, as well as the consideration of using specific techniques to help engage client into treatment (e.g., psychoeducation, motivational interviewing).

Example questions:
- How do you explain what you are struggling/coping with?
- How do you make sense of your particular situation?
- What are your expectations about treatment (e.g., frequency, duration, approach, goals, and desired outcome)?
- What are your expectations from this therapeutic relationship (e.g., structure of therapy, availability of the therapist)?
- What do you feel is most challenging for you right now?
- What do you believe are your most important areas of strength?
- How satisfied are you with the most important relationships in your life? What role have you played in creating/maintaining these dynamics?
- If we were successful with treatment, how would your life change? Can you give me examples?
- How do you feel about change?

Clinician-Related and Contextual Variables

The last area that must be assessed involves the clinical competencies of professionalism and reflective practice. Professionalism refers to the clinician's integrity and accountability, their deportment, their concern for the welfare of others, as well as their professional identity. As such, the clinician is expected to monitor and address potential issues within the assessment process that can challenge his/her professional values and integrity to ensure the client receives the best quality of care. It also means that the clinician is expected to act to safeguard the welfare of his client, through the appropriate demonstration of his/her knowledge and know-how about issues related to the assessment, diagnosis, and treatment of presenting concerns, thus integrating science and practice to effect evidence-based care. In addition, reflective practice refers to the ability to display self-awareness and mindfulness about professional practice, how his/her own worldview, competencies and limitations may influence care, as well as to show understanding of the contextual variables that can affect treatment delivery (e.g., institutional systems, financial constraints, issues related to power and diversity).

Examples questions:
- What is the level of professional training needed to address this difficulty?
- What approach should be used, and what is the clinician's level of competence in this approach?
- How might the clinician's culture, worldview, and spirituality /religion influence the therapy process?
- Based on available clinical expertise and judgment, what would be considered most important to address in therapy to optimize outcomes?
- Should the clinician seek out supervision or other support (consultation) for this case?
- Based on a broad scope of research (e.g., RCT, meta-analysis, case studies, qualitative studies), what is the best approach to use with this client given his/her presenting problems, and his/her goals and preferences?

- Are there any constraints on the number of sessions being offered because of third-party involvement or the client's preferences/resources available to them?
- Are there any constraints on the therapeutic approach being used in the particular clinical setting where the assessment is taking place?
- If the client's needs are outside of the clinician's specific context of service delivery, what other resources are available that may better suit the client's needs?

Case Formulation Framework

A case formulation is a statement that helps to conceptualize the information obtained during the course of a psychological assessment, to present the potential causes and nature of the presenting concerns, which is usually accompanied by a psychological diagnosis, if appropriate. A good case formulation should be (1) clear and parsimonious (i.e., it is internally consistent, understandable; and its key concepts are specific and nonredundant), (2) precise and testable (i.e., it presents testable hypotheses with measurable concepts), (3) empirically adequate (i.e., the mechanisms posited are based on empirical evidence), (4) comprehensive and generalizable (i.e., the model used is general enough to be used for various clinical phenomena), and (5) useful and applied enough (i.e., it is useful in communicating with the client, and interventions based on the use of the model have demonstrated efficacy) (Dawson and Moghaddam, 2016).

Based on the psychological assessment structure we presented earlier, we can now create a case formulation framework that is both concise and focused on the core presenting issues, the main factors at play, and the areas of priority for diagnosis and treatment recommendations.

First, the clinician presents the reason for consultation and what prompted seeking services at this particular time. Then, presenting concerns are summarized, including their onset, duration, severity, and chronicity. Attempts to cope with, mitigate, or treat presenting symptoms are exposed, including current resources used by the person to cope with these concerns.

Second, predisposing and precipitating factors are explained, including factors that maintain, decrease, or increase their severity over time. Main stressors are highlighted, and their potential impact on symptoms is posited. Associated background information that is relevant to the presenting concerns is summarized, including the impact of symptoms on the main areas of functioning in the person's life, including work/school, immediate family, and interpersonal relationships more generally.

Third, ecosystemic factors of relevance are presented and in particular, any potential issues related to marginalization, acculturation, and victimization to help contextualize presenting concerns within a larger sociocultural and economic context. Potential barriers to identify and access resources are also identified. Psychological diagnosis is made if and when appropriate.

Fourth, recommendations for the inclusion of other health professionals within the circle of care, as well as any other community resources are presented and justified in light of the current clinical case conceptualization (including main symptoms identified, as well as diagnosis if appropriate). Finally, potential limitations and prognostic concerns are highlighted to guide the drafting of treatment recommendations.

In the next chapter, we will provide a case vignette to demonstrate the use of this model for completing a psychological assessment and drafting of a case formulation, using our model.

References

Anderson, N. B. (2006). Evidence-based practice in psychology: American Psychological Association Presidential Task Force on evidence-based practice. *American Psychologist, 61*(4), 271–285.

Brofenbrenner, U. (1979). *The ecological of human development : Experiments by nature and design.* Cambridge, MA: Harvard University Press.

Dawson, D. L., and Moghaddam, N. G. (2016). Formulation in action: An introduction. In D. L. Dawson, and N. G. Moghaddam (Eds.), *Formulation in action: Applying psychological theory to clinical practice* (pp. 3–8). New York, NY: Walter de Gruyter.

Di Blasi, Z., Harkness, E., Ernst, E., Georgiou, A., and Kleijnen, J. (2001). Influence of context effects on health outcomes: A systematic review. *The Lancet, 357*(9258), 757–762.

Haynes, S. N., Smith, G. T., and Hunsley, J. D. (2011). *Scientific foundations of clinical assessment*. New York, NY: Routledge Taylor and Francis Group.

Hunsley, J., and Mash, E. J. (2008). *A guide to assessments that work*. London, UK: Oxford University Press.

Lambert, M. J. (2013). *Bergin and Garfield's handbook of psychotherapy and behavior change* (6th ed.). Hoboken, NJ: John Wiley and Sons.

Nathan, P. E., and Gorman, J. M. (2007). *A guide to treatments that work*. London, UK: Oxford University Press.

Norcross, J. C. (2011). *Psychotherapy relationships that work: Evidence-based responsiveness* (2nd ed.). London, UK: Oxford Press.

Zimmerman, M. (2013). Interview Guide For Evaluating DSM-5 Psychiatric Disorders and the Mental Status Examination (2nd ed.), East Greenwich, RI: Psych Products Press.

CHAPTER 4

Conducting Psychological Assessment and Creating a Case Formulation

In Chapter 3, we learned about an evidence-based, integrative, and interprofessional model for psychological assessment that comprised six areas of inquiry. In this chapter, we will present a clinical vignette to illustrate how this model can be used in the context of a psychological assessment session. We will begin by introducing basic information and initial impressions provided by the referral agent, and then we will focus on each area of inquiry, including examples of clinician–patient interactions to illustrate how relevant information can be obtained throughout the psychological assessment process.

Clinical Case Vignette

You are a clinical psychologist working in a primary care setting in a rural area outside a large urban center. Patients are often referred to you by the family physicians at the clinic where you practice when they suspect that their patients could benefit from psychological services or when they have queries regarding the mental health of the patients they are currently treating for physical concerns. The person you are about to assess is typical of the patients seen at the clinic.

Mr. Dwight Scranton, 57-year-old, lives with his wife (aged 55 years) and two children (aged 20 and 25 years) in this rural area. For the past 25 years, he has worked as a foreman for a midsize paper company. His family physician referred him to help him cope with symptoms of anxiety and depression that appeared shortly after Mr. Scranton's heart attack 6 months ago. Upon contacting him, Mr. Scranton agrees to meet with you and arrives on time for his appointment. He is clean-shaven and dressed in loose fitting clothes to accommodate an overweight frame. He appears willing and able to participate fully in the assessment process, although he denotes that his doctor must think "he is crazy if he thought a shrink was needed" before apologizing for his comment.

Symptoms

Upon initial inquiry about his presenting concerns, Mr. Scranton endorses the presence of the following depressive symptoms: low mood, significant decrease in interest for pleasurable activities, sleep disturbances (i.e., frequent awakenings, breathing pauses, and restless nights), decrease in libido, memory and concentration difficulties, and a significant increase in irritability. He does not report current suicidal ideations. He also notes being more aware of his physical sensations (e.g., his heart rate) since his last heart attack and endorses the presence of intense periods of panic (both unexpected and situation-bound) accompanied by the following symptoms: palpitations, shortness of breath, tightness in his chest, excessive sweating, intense fear of dying, or having another heart attack. He indicates that his symptoms are having a detrimental impact on his quality of life, especially in the context of his relationship with his wife and work performance.

Interview excerpt

Clinician: How about we start with you telling me about some of the stressors you have been coping with?

Mr. Scranton: Sure, well like I told Dr. Sobel, it's been a bit of a rough time since the heart attack. I'm just feeling on edge a lot, not sleeping well. More heartburn too, sometimes I worry I'm having another one (*heart attack*)! It just gets you to think, you know, there's more life behind you than in front.

C: Can you tell me more about that? What does that mean in your day-to-day activities?

S: I just don't care as much as I did I guess, about what I use to like. For example, I spend more time flipping through channels than watching anything on TV. It drives my wife insane! Then we get into these arguments, and I just don't want to do that, because I can feel my heart, you know, beating in my chest. It just, it just . . . I don't want it to happen again.

C: So you mentioned arguments with you wife. How often do these happen?

S: Oh, I don't know, all the time. At work too. I just have no patience anymore. No patience. . . .

C: Can you tell me more about that?

S: You know how it is, everyone thinks they know best. For a long time, I would try to make everyone happy, avoid creating problems. I just don't have the patience anymore to referee all their little squabbles. Life is too short, and I just don't care anymore.

C: You don't care anymore. What did you care about, before all this happened?

S: Well, work, family, the big things. It's just that with what happened, you start to think you work hard for 30 years, getting close to retirement, and then this happens out of nowhere. It can just be all taken away, and who would miss you really? I don't like to talk about this stuff (*looks down as he appears to compose himself*).

C: Mr. Scranton, I wonder if we can go back a bit to what you said about feeling on edge. What does that look like? Can you give me an example?

S: Sure. I just feel like I'm more aware of everything in my body, like I'm tuned in 24/7. I can hear my heart beat. It's disturbing and tiring. I just wish I could turn it off. I can't sleep at night. The slightest noise wakes me. Sometimes it feels like I stop breathing or something. Scares the heck out of me! It just makes me irritable, like anything can set me off. And when it does, boy!

C: What do you mean by setting you off? Can you help me understand?

S: It's just that sometimes I know it's going to happen, like I can feel it coming on, but sometimes it just happens. Feels like I'm dying again. I just can't breathe, hard as I may try. I just, I'm afraid to lose control. Lose my mind . . . Lose just everything . . .

C: So you have these moments of, can I call it panic?

S: Yeah, sure.

C: Okay, so you have these moments of panic—sometimes you can feel it coming on, but sometimes not—and you have trouble breathing. Is there anything else that happens in those moments?

S: Well, I can feel my heart beating out of my chest for one thing. I just start sweating like a pig (*chuckles nervously*). I'm no pretty sight, I can tell you that.

C: So that must be very scary for you.

S: Yeah, yeah, I think I'm dying every time. Until I can calm myself down, but then I'm just exhausted afterwards.

C: Of course. I can understand that. How often do these episodes occur?

S: At least once a week.

Personal History

Mr. Scranton reports a happy childhood. He grew up in the same area that he lives in now with his parents and three siblings. He describes his father as a somewhat distant parental figure who expressed few emotions, but who was a role model and provided well for their family. He passed away at the age of 60 years from a heart attack. His mother was a homemaker. He describes her as a hard worker with a nervous disposition. She suffered a stroke 2 years ago and is still alive. Mr. Scranton reports having relatively good relationships with his colleagues at work, but his relationship with his superior is difficult. Mr. Scranton feels a great deal of pressure from him, and this has been going on for a long time. Mr. Scranton reports coping with stress by having a drink at night and on the weekend, or by chatting with his colleagues during breaks, or doing a family activity. Mr. Scranton is presently overweight, and his weight gain has increased particularly over the past 10 years, following a promotion at work that took him off the floor and into office work. He suffers from hypertension and high cholesterol. Finally, he reports erectile dysfunction, which he refuses to discuss with his family doctor or his wife.

Interview excerpt

Clinician: Can you tell me a bit more about your background? Did you grow up around here?

Mr. Scranton: Yeah, I did. Eldest of four kids. My dad worked at the mill too. My mother stayed at home to watch us kids, but she did a bit of sewing for the neighbors. She was always worried about money. She didn't want us to go without. A real worrywart!

C: What was it like at home?

S: When I was a boy? Well, I'm sure it was the way it was for most folks. My father worked long hours and expected his meal ready when he got home. He wasn't around much, but we always had what we needed, and he was there when it mattered. He was a good man, solid. I was expected to help out, being the eldest. I often was the one who had to keep my siblings in check, and I also got blamed if something happened. I didn't mind it too much, when you are older you need to take responsibility for the younger ones. I wasn't too good in school. I just felt bored a lot. Preferred to work with my hands; so I started at the mill when I was maybe 18 and that was it.

C: How do you like your work?

S: It's fine. I liked working with the guys. There was good camaraderie. About 10 years ago, there was an opening for a shift manager. I applied more as a lark. I didn't really think they'd pick me. I don't even have my high school diploma. But here we are!

C: How do you find your new position?

S: It's okay. I was getting used to it I guess. The biggest issue is my boss. He can be really controlling. I saw him do the same to the previous guy. I'm pretty sure that's why he decided to take early retirement. He just couldn't stand him no [sic] more. Maybe I would have been better off staying on the floor, not moving to the offices.

C: Why is that? Can you tell me more about that?

S: I just miss it sometimes. I still have a good relationship with most guys, but now I have to keep them in line. I can't joke all the time. And they all come to me with their problems. I got this boss on one side always on my back and then the guys on the other with their squabbles and their favors and what not.

C: It sounds like it can be a bit overwhelming sometimes?

S: Yes, yes, it is. I just feel, you know, this tightness in my throat or my chest sometimes. Maybe that's where the heart attack comes from . . .

C: What do you do to cope with the stress? Can you turn to your wife for support?

S: Ahh, I just go home and I'll pour myself a rum and coke. Maybe a couple on the weekends. I don't talk much to my wife about it. She can't really help.

C: What about turning to her for comfort when you are feeling stressed?

S: I guess so. But we haven't been intimate in a long time. She gets mad at me for it; so I usually try to avoid her a bit. You know?

C: You say you haven't been intimate in a while. Do you have a sense of why that might be?

S: Yes, yeah I know. I just don't like to talk about that kind of thing. It's embarrassing (*looks down at the floor*).

C: Does she know that you are experiencing difficulty with . . .

S: NO! Absolutely not. Sorry, I didn't mean to speak loudly. I'm just not comfortable talking about it with her.

C: Have you talked about it with anyone else, perhaps Dr. Sobel?

S: No, no I haven't and I won't. It's no one's business but my own.

Ecosystemic Factors

Mr. Scranton reports that he receives adequate support from his spouse and children. However, the emotional intimacy in his relationship with his wife has decreased over recent years because of his erectile dysfunction and his avoidance of the subject matter in his interactions with his wife. His social network includes a few work colleagues, a few childhood friends, and his extended family. Although this is a relatively rich network, Mr. Scranton does not confide much in others and does not easily ask for help. He reports that his wife watches over him more since he had his heart attack. She tells him to work less and eat better, which he finds irritating. The stress at work has not decreased since his heart attack, and he does not feel that he can retire now, because of a few financial stressors he is coping with. Mr. Scranton lives in a rural area where there are few grocery stores that offer fresh produce and quality ingredients. This results in him eating more fast food, because it is more easily accessible given his work shift schedule.

Interview excerpt

Clinician: I wonder if we could talk a bit more about current stressors and how you are coping with them. You mentioned that your wife suggested that you work less hours, but you said this is not an option right now, correct?

Mr. Scranton: Yes, she just doesn't understand sometimes. Money doesn't grow on trees you know. I have a daughter in university and a son who just got laid off. I am helping him pay his mortgage for now, and I'm also supporting my daughter. It can be really hard for kids now to get started in life, certainly isn't like it was when I was their age. I can't take an early retirement, and my job is not the kind of work where I can just decide to work less. I have a schedule. I have to be there for my shift, and that is that.

C: Sometimes when we are under stress, there are ways for us to limit the stress. Other times, however, the stress is not something we have much control over, but what we do have control over is how we cope with it. I wonder who you can turn to when you are feeling stressed and you need to unwind?

S: I guess I usually go and chat with a couple of my buddies at the mill. We all started around the same time; so we've been through a lot together. Sometimes it's just about cracking a couple jokes in the break room. It can really help take your mind off things for a minute. Sometimes I'll also grab a pint with a friend when we meet to watch the game at the pub. Although it's been harder to meet up recently. He is a grandfather now and is spending more time with his grandchildren.

C: Are you able to talk about what stresses you with these friends or with anyone else?

S: Well, I don't want to bother people. I find it's good to just try and find something to laugh at for a bit, to take the edge off. I don't want them to think I can't handle myself. Everyone's already treating me with kid's gloves since the heart attack. And I would never talk about this with my kids. That's not their role.

C: Is there anything that you do that makes you feel better when you're upset or feeling down?

S: Well, if it gets to be too much, I'll just take a break and drive to the local coffee shop for a cruller. Have you ever had one? Oh my, are they ever good! So yeah, sometimes I'll go and just get one or a couple. Sometimes I also get upset with the lunches my wife is packing me: a salad with a couple of crackers. I'll eat the thing in two seconds, and I'm hungry again within a minute. So, I'll run to the fast food joint up the road from the mill and just order something.

C: Is there anything else that you can do, such as taking a walk, listening to music, relaxing?

S: Well, I guess sometimes I'll put on an old movie and doze off in front of the TV.

Interdisciplinary Collaboration

Mr. Scranton reports smoking a pack of cigarettes per day. He also consumes one to two rum and cokes per day, and approximately five to ten beers per day over the weekend. His lifestyle is mostly sedentary, and he does not participate in physical activities for fear of causing another heart attack. His diet lacks variety and isn't balanced (e.g., he eats few vegetables and a lot of meat). He was referred by his family doctor to a cardiac rehab program offered at the clinic, and he is followed by a cardiologist. Finally, he has had the same family doctor for more than 15 years, but often finds that there is not enough time to talk about what is troubling him during his medical appointment. His current medications include Nitroglycerin (Spray), Atorvastatin (80 mg po qd), Candesartan (16 mg po qd), and Citalopram (30mg po qd).

Interview excerpt

Clinician: I see here in your chart that you are a smoker. Are you still smoking about a pack a day?

Mr. Scranton: Yes, for the last 30 years. Started when I was new at the mill. It was a good way to make friends, going off on smoke breaks. I tried to quit a couple of times, but I just can't kick the habit. Now, I find that if I try to stop, I just get even more on edge, so I don't, but I do worry that it's no good for my heart.

C: Is that something you would like to work on if we could help with the withdrawal symptoms?

S: Yeah, sure, maybe. Whatever you think might help.

C: I also see here that you are taking a few medications for blood pressure, angina, cholesterol, and an antidepressant. How is these working for you?

S: Fine I guess. I take the Atorvastatin; so I'm not too worried about what I eat. Candesartan is fine, and I take the Nitroglycerin spray when I feel like I might have symptoms starting so I can nip that in the bud before it can really start.

C: So you take the Nitroglycerin more preventively then?

S: Yes, that's right. I know the cardiologist said I should wait till I have chest pains, but I'm not taking that risk!

C: Hmm, okay. What about your antidepressant, Citalopram?

S: I take that when I feel like I might need it. I try not to abuse it.

C: So you don't take it regularly?

S: No, no I don't want to get dependent on it.

C: Did Dr. Sobel and you talk about how and when to take your medications for it to be most effective?

S: Oh, I don't know, maybe. Dr. Sobel is really busy, and he often runs out before I can him questions. I think he explained it to me. In any case, I can figure it out on my own.

C: Dr. Sobel has been your family doctor for a while now. Do you feel comfortable talking with him?

S: Yes, of course. I mean I wish he had more time to talk when I see him. You know how it is: he asks me if [I] have any questions, but before I can really think about it, he just says okay then! That's it and he's off. He's a nice guy, real professional. I don't want you to think I'm badmouthing him.

C: Not at all. I am interested in gaining a better understanding of the other health professionals within your circle of care, the type of role they play in managing your overall health, and how that is working for you.

S: Oh, okay. Sounds good.

C: What about your cardiologist, Dr. Amin? What is she like?

S: She's fine. She seems a bit young to be a doctor, but she looks like she really knows her stuff. I have a friend who also sees her, and he thinks she's great, so you know I trust her.

Prognostic Considerations

Mr. Scranton appears to have little insight into the relationship that exists between his thoughts, his feelings, and his behavior. At the same time, he does understand that his heart attack contributed to his current difficulties. He shows some motivation to improve his current overall well-being when asked directly about his goal for treatment, but does not seem ready to change current habits that are maintaining presenting issues. As a result, he presents with a level of ambivalence toward his overall engagement in both participating in a cardiac rehab program and obtaining psychological services to help him manage symptoms of depression and anxiety.

Interview excerpt

Clinician: We talked about a number of issues that you have been coping with. Were these issues, the panic attacks, the loss of interest, and the insomnia, to name a few, were they present before your heart attack?

Mr. Scranton: No, no I don't think so. I feel like something changed when I had the heart attack. I feel a bit like I'm a different person sometimes. I don't know, maybe I was naïve you know?

C: Naïve how?

S: Oh, I guess I thought things would be okay. I thought I was stronger than that.

C: The heart attack has left you feeling more vulnerable.

S: I don't know about that. I mean I'm not out there crying by myself. I just mean that there is sort of life before the heart attack, and then life after. The two are just not the same.

C: Okay, we have talked about how both your cardiologist and your family doctor recommended a few changes to your lifestyle to help you manage your overall health. I am getting the sense though that this isn't a plan that is sitting well with you. Is that correct?

S: It's just that they seem to think it's so easy. Just eat better they say. Go for a walk. Join a gym. I don't have time for all that, and I don't like salad! Besides, if I start doing more physical activity, my heart starts acting up. I'm not risking another heart attack just so they can feel good about ensuring I follow their advice. I have been putting on my pants one leg at a time by myself for over 50 years. I think I know what's best for me.

C: Alright, I really appreciate how straightforward you are with me. I can tell that you are a person that is used to taking charge when needed. That's good. At the same time, how do you see us working together to help you improve your coping with what has been troubling you?

S: I don't know. I have never seen a psychologist before. You aren't exactly what I expected. It seems pretty easy to talk to you. I do want to make things better. I'd like to sleep better, to enjoy doing things again. I'd like for the panic attacks to stop. It's a real nuisance. I don't know what you can do about it, but I am willing to hear what you have to suggest.

Clinician-Related and Contextual Variables

Mr. Scranton is a middle-aged man living in a rural area. He has limited education and overall poor life hygiene habits. Working with him will require engaging him in the therapeutic process to ensure that he commits to making some much-needed changes. There is a risk for the working alliance to be more difficult to establish, because of differences in background, as well as ambivalence toward treatment. As such, the therapeutic process may be affected by countertransference surrounding treatment priorities and objectives. In addition, given that the patient lives in a rural area and that he engages in shift work, there may be a number of contextual barriers that will limit his ability to make effective changes to his lifestyle. These barriers may add further frustration to the therapeutic relationship. Finally, given that Mr. Scranton is following by his family doctor, his cardiologist, and has recently been referred to a cardiac rehab program, psychological treatment will need to be coordinated with other forms of ongoing treatment. It may also be necessary for the clinician to help educate Mr. Scranton about the value of these other parts of his treatment to help him engage in the process (e.g., cardiac rehab), as well as educate him about proper use of medication to maximize efficacy and prevent the further exacerbation of current health issues.

Interview excerpt

Clinician: Mr. Scranton, I really appreciate you taking the time to meet with me today. I see myself as a part of your health management team. As such, I think it's important to see how the work we might do together will fit with the other services you are receiving here at the clinic and in the community. I think we also really need to reflect on what is most important at this time for you to feel better overall and also to feel more in control of your health. Does that make sense?

Mr. Scranton: Yeah, yeah for sure. I like the sound of that.

C: I am glad to hear it. For us to work effectively together, I think that we need to agree on what we need to focus our attention on, and we might need to problem-solve a bit around any barriers we might encounter that would make it difficult for you to succeed in whatever plan we set up.

S: Okay, that makes sense.

C: Great, so perhaps you can help me now by telling me, if we were successful in our work together, how might things be different? How would we know that it worked?

S: I don't really know. I guess it's what I said before: I would sleep better. I wouldn't feel on edge all the time, and I would enjoy things more. Maybe I'd be a little less angry.

C: Angry?

S: Yeah, I think I feel angry a lot. I mean I don't yell at anyone or anything like that, but I feel it.

C: Okay, that is good information for me to know. I think it makes a lot of sense that you might feel angry, and also sad and maybe even a little afraid sometimes. What has happened to you can be deeply unsettling, and it's also forced you to reassess a lot about your life: your job, your eating habits, and your routine. All this can be pretty overwhelming especially when we are used to being in control of our life.

S: Yeah, that's right. You just hit the nail on the head.

Case Formulation for Mr. Scranton

Mr. Scranton is a married, overweight, middle-aged paper mill shift supervisor who recently suffered a heart attack (*patient identifying information*). He presents with moderate depressive and anxious symptoms, including regular panic attacks (*reason for consultation*). He was referred for a psychological assessment by his family doctor, at the same time that he was referred to a cardiac rehab program at his family medicine clinic. Mr. Scranton reports that his current depressive and anxious symptoms appeared mainly after his heart attack, although he recalled feeling chest pains and stress symptoms at work prior to his heart attack. His current symptoms are present on a daily basis and have a negative impact on his quality of life: he has lost interest in things he previously enjoyed, he does not sleep well, he often feels overwhelmed, and he feels constantly "on edge." As a result, he has noticed an increase in conflicts in his relationship with his wife and with his coworkers (*summary of presenting concerns*). His main coping mechanisms include isolating himself or using distraction. Although Mr. Scranton reports benefitting from a rich social network (spouse, adult children, extended family, coworkers, childhood friends), he refuses to seek their help because he does not want to burden others with his problems and feels strongly that it is his responsibility to manage his concerns himself (*attempts to cope*).

Mr. Scranton leads a mostly sedentary lifestyle. He engages in very few physical activities and is a heavy smoker. He reports feeling fearful that engaging in exercise may put him at risk of another heart attack. His prior attempts to quit smoking have been unsuccessful, and so he shows little motivation to try again. His diet can be labeled as traditional, and he frequently consumes fast food (*predisposing and precipitation factors*). Living in a rural area, he does not benefit from easy access to healthy meal options and has shown resistance to changes in his diet suggested by his wife and his family doctor (*maintaining factors*).

Mr. Scranton presents with a number of stressors in his life (*ecosystemic factors*). He reports having a conflictual relationship with his superior at work, who he perceives as overcontrolling and demanding. He also reports frequent disagreements with his wife concerning his lifestyle and their lack of intimacy. The latter appears partly caused by Mr. Scranton's erectile dysfunction, an issue he has kept secret so far and is adamant is not discussed with either his wife or his family doctor. Finally, he also reports some financial concerns relating to supporting both his adult children as they complete their postsecondary education and cope with a recent job loss.

Mr. Scranton grew up in this rural area (*associated background information*). He was the eldest of four siblings. His father worked at the same paper mill where he is currently employed. It appears that Mr. Scranton was heavily influenced by his father in how he defines himself as a man, worker, and father (i.e., it is important to be self-reliant, you must take responsibility for your actions, and you must work hard). In addition, he also appears to have internalized expectations put forth at home in his role as the first born (e.g., it is important to take care of others, you should not burden those in your care with your troubles, and you are expected to be in control). As a result, Mr. Scranton does not seek support, does not easily show vulnerability, and feels a strong sense of duty toward his family, and an expectation that he must appear in control of his life (*potential barriers*).

Mr. Scranton presents with symptoms that are consistent with a diagnosis of adjustment disorder with depressive symptoms and panic disorder (*diagnostic considerations*). Although Mr. Scranton reported some stress-related symptoms prior to his heart attack, it seems that these were not the cause of any preexisting mental disorder. Given the nature of his current difficulties and how these are related to his recent heart attack, it will be important for psychological treatment to be coordinated with his cardiac rehab program, and ongoing monitoring by his family doctor. In addition, if these resources are not part of the cardiac rehab program, it may be useful to consider a referral to a registered dietician and a kinesiologist to help Mr. Scranton improve his eating and physical activity (*inclusion of other health professionals within circle of care*).

Given his current ambivalence toward making changes to his habits and routine, it will be crucial to prioritize developing motivation and mobilization for change as first step in the treatment process. Potential barriers to accessing relevant services and resources should also be queried early in the treatment process and reassessed regularly to maintain momentum toward meeting treatment objectives. In addition, it will be very important to engage Mr. Scranton as a central player in his recovery plan, so that he can feel invested in the treatment process and to ensure legitimacy and relevance of treatment goals (*prognostic concerns*).

CHAPTER 5

An Integrative Interprofessional Model for Psychological Treatment Planning and Monitoring

In Chapters 3 and 4, we introduced an integrative model for assessment based on the common factors, literature and theoretical integration design, to fit a wide range of presentation and contexts, regardless of the specific orientation of the clinician. The next two chapters will focus on treatment planning and delivery. As for the assessment chapters, we make the assumption that the reader already possesses the required clinical skills to deliver mental health services. Therefore, the model presented here should not be seen as a treatment model per se, but as a general framework that can be useful to guide intervention planning and monitoring. As mentioned in the first chapters, it is always the responsibility of clinicians to make sure that their practice is evidence-based (i.e., that they have consulted the most pertinent research, used their clinical expertise, and considered relevant client- and context-centered variables). This chapter starts with a description of the theoretical and empirical underpinnings of our integrative interprofessional treatment model and the spheres included in it. Next, we introduce important questions clinicians should ask themselves in order to identify treatment priorities and targets. Special attention will be given to treatment outcome and alliance monitoring throughout service delivery.

We are very sensitive to the idea that integrative practice should not fall in the same trap that many psychological approaches have fallen into, which is to develop numerous integrative models that promise to deliver something unique and different from other approaches. We want to make clear that our model is not "unique." As you will read in the next section, other models exist and should be considered. We do not see our model as a replacement to other evidence-based treatment (EBT) models but more as a general framework that allows the clinician to use the different EBT models at his/her disposal in a more systematic and integrative manner. The originality of our model is that it helps organize the treatment plan by focusing on three spheres (i.e., Capacity, Mastery and Competence of Self, Mastery and Competence with Others) that can include multiple components consistent with other models or approaches (for example, thoughts, emotions, physical sensations, and behaviors). By orienting the treatment plan within three spheres or targets, it simplifies the process for both the clinician and the client by introducing a simple and common language to treatment delivery. We also add to previous treatment planning models by integrating the notion of interprofessional collaboration and context-specific variables to better reflect the real-life decisions that clinicians need to take into account when planning and offering psychological services.

Other Integrative Models

Before we introduce our framework, it seems important to discuss other models that have already been developed. The Transtheoretical Model of Prochaska and DiClemente (1984, 2005) is a good example. Central to this model are four dimensions: (1) the process of change, (2) the stages of change, (3) the pros and cons of change, and (4) levels of change (Prochaska and DiClemente, 2005). It posits that the selection of interventions should not be predetermined but tailored to the client's stage of change (i.e., precontemplation, contemplation, preparation, action, and maintenance) because the processes of change that can help an individual move from one stage to another vary accordingly. The desired level of change should also be considered to plan and deliver fruitful interventions (i.e., symptom/situational problems, maladaptive cognitions, current interpersonal conflicts, family/system conflicts, and interpersonal conflicts). See Prochaska and DiClemente (2005) for a more detailed review.

More recently, Brooks-Harris (2008) developed a Multitheoretical Therapy Framework combining seven approaches (i.e., experiential, cognitive, behavioral, biopsychosocial, systemic, psychodynamic, and multicultural). This framework rests on five guiding principles that exemplify what integrative psychotherapy should be (i.e., intentional, multidimensional, multitheoretical, strategy-based, and relational). Using five specific steps and various treatment resources (e.g., the Focus Marker Checklist, Multidimensional Survey, Multitheoretical Conceptualization, and Catalog of Key Strategies), therapists can observe and assess seven dimensions based on their client's presenting concerns, collaboratively target with the client two or three dimensions on which to focus treatment (i.e., focal dimension), formulate a multitheoretical conceptualization, and choose related intervention strategies from the seven theoretical approaches mentioned earlier. The focal dimensions identified in the Multidimensional Model of Human Functioning are: (1) thoughts, (2) feelings, (3) actions, (4) biology, (5) interpersonal patterns, (6) social systems, and (7) cultural contexts. This model centers on the interrelations between thoughts, emotions, and actions (i.e., concurrent dimensions of functioning) that can generate psychopathology as well as the broader contextual factors that the client needs (or needed) to adapt to (i.e., contextual dimensions of functioning). Key strategies are selected from a catalog of approximately 100 strategies based on the client's characteristics and case conceptualization. You can learn more at: www.multitheoretical.com or read the *Integrative Multitheoretical Psychotherapy* textbook (Brooks-Harris, 2008). In her integrative model, Jones-Smith (2012) adds to Brook-Harris (2008)'s model by including the following spheres: evidence-based research or empirical support for counseling interventions, change process, and strengths-internal/external. Interestingly, in conjunction with the presentation of his integrative model, Jones-Smith (2012) suggests guidelines (or important questions) for clinicians wishing to develop their own integrative framework.

Finally, Holm-Hadulla, Hofmann, and Sperth (2011) elaborated the ABCDE model of integrative counseling based on client-centered, cognitive behavioral, and psychodynamic existential approaches. The ABCDE stands for alliance, behaviors, cognition, dynamics, and existentials. The metatheoretical framework they utilize is modern hermeneutics, suggesting that psychotherapy does not happen in a vacuum but in the context of a relationship/communication between the client and the clinician. Each part of the model is seen as influencing each other through a process of reciprocity. Special attention is given to the strengths and resources of the client. They also describe their model as solution-focused.

What we especially like about these models is that the authors emphasize that the development of an integrative approach should be done *intentionally* and *collaboratively* (see Brooks-Harris, 2008 or Jones-Smith, 2012). These are characteristics that have also driven the development of the treatment planning and monitoring framework that we will present here. Regardless of the model you choose, it is important to keep these two key concepts in mind. Practicing psychotherapy is a privilege; we have to be thorough and informed about the choices we make based on the best available research and clinical expertise, while ensuring that the treatment delivered is flexible and tailored to the individual and context.

Description of the Integrative Interprofessional Model for Psychological Treatment Planning and Monitoring

Relational/Attachment-based

First, our model rests on client-centered approaches (e.g., Rogers, 1961, 1992), and process-experiential approaches (e.g., Elliott, Watson, Goldman, and Greenberg, 2004; Greenberg, Rice, and Elliott, 1993) principles, and is embedded within an attachment framework. Collaboration, mutual understanding of the treatment goals, and the offer of an accepting presence are all important elements, but research on attachment deepens and reinforces the importance of being attuned to the client's experience (Bowlby, 1969, 1988; Cassidy and Shaver, 2008). Through the complex process of empathic attunement (see Elliott et al., 2004 for a more detailed description), clinicians help to create the emotional safety needed for the client to explore their inner experience and generate a more coherent narrative of themselves, others, and the world as well as develop their capacity for emotion regulation, adaptive action, and open communication (see Costello, 2013). As Wylie and Turner (2011) noted, "rather than recoiling from the intensity of the client's experience, the therapist is providing—through voice tone, eye contact, expression, posture, as well as words—the stability, the ballast, so to speak, to keep the client feeling not only understood, but safely held and supported" (p. 6). The therapeutic relationship acts as a safe haven and secure base for the client by being sensitive and responsive (Johnson, 2009). As an active companion, the clinician provides a felt security to the client (Costello, 2013). Given as the well-established research evidence on alliance and its impact on therapeutic outcome (see Wampold and Imel, 2015), we cannot emphasize enough that the relational context in which therapy takes place needs to be at the forefront of the treatment process. We do not view empathy, attunement, unconditional positive regard, authenticity, congruence, presence, and acceptance as "techniques" but as a necessary stance that clinicians have to take when offering services. It is a way of "being with" the client that is necessary for successful therapeutic work to occur.

Evidence-based

Second, our model is grounded in an evidence base that includes the best research available from a variety of sources (not limited to RCTs), as well as clinician- and client-centered variables. It not only makes room for clinical judgment and the clinical acumen in making decisions about what/when/with whom to apply certain strategies and techniques, but also implies that clinicians are responsible to regularly consult the best available research, and continue to keep up with important findings in their field of practice regardless of their level of experience or expertise.

Strength-based

Third, we begin by recognizing that our clients did what they needed to in order to adapt to their life circumstances. We do not take the position that individuals develop "distorted" cognitions or perceptions out of the blue and are therefore irrational beings. If you were repeatedly abused by your father when growing up, it makes sense to see the world as a dangerous place and to find it difficult to trust others. Actually, it was probably smart to develop these worldviews. Nevertheless, when used rigidly and without flexibility, these rules or assumptions can become problematic. Said differently, we see the client as having developed strategies to cope the best way they could with the available resources at hand. If the client is in your office right now, he/she must have done something right and have inner resources/strengths that need to be highlighted and capitalized on. This underpinning also speaks to our view that clients are not individuals in need of "fixing" or "saving." They are an equal collaborator in the treatment process. Therefore, when treating individuals using this model, clinicians need to make frequent check-ins with the client (e.g., "Does this make sense to you? Does this fit with your experience? Does that resonate with what is going on for you right now?).

Accountable

Fourth, our model takes into consideration the importance of being accountable to clients. Monitoring outcomes and the ongoing impact of interventions from the client's perspective is important because research has shown that clinicians are often poor judges of their client's progress or deterioration (see Lambert, 2013) and often overestimate the efficacy of their interventions (Walfish, McAlister, O'Donnell, and Lambert, 2012). Therefore, from the start of treatment, clinicians need to determine how they will monitor treatment outcomes. Openness to feedback seems a crucial element of any treatment plan. As discussed in earlier chapters, a multitude of tools are available (e.g., OQ-45, PCOMS, CORE). Alternatively, accountability can also take the form of self-reflection and deliberate practice. It can be reflected in your ability to: (1) own your contribution to the therapeutic process (good or bad), (2) be attentive to breaks in the therapeutic alliance, and (3) be sensitive to countertransference issues and your own experience when delivering services, which are all essential ingredients to being an effective therapist (Lecomte et al., 2004; Miller, Hubble, and Duncan, 2008; Skovholt and Jennings, 2004).

Treatment Spheres

Following the assessment and case formulation phase, the clinician should have obtained sufficient information to create a broad picture of the client's life situation and the client's ability to engage in an integrative psychological treatment plan. Although our model includes dimensions similar to the ones presented in other models and frameworks mentioned earlier in this chapter, including individual variables (thoughts, emotions, behaviors, body/physical sensations, spirituality/religion), relational or interpersonal components, as well as broader contextual and cultural factors, we have organized these dimensions into three broader treatment spheres: (1) Capacity, (2) Mastery and Competence of Self, and (3) Mastery and Competence with Others. This is because it seems difficult to see all these different dimensions (e.g., thoughts, emotions, behaviors, and relationships) as silos or distinct and mutually exclusive targets, because they inherently interact with one another and it can be difficult to determine in what category your client experience and reactions falls into. For these reasons, we have focused on three treatment targets that can guide treatment planning and streamline the treatment plan to facilitate presenting treatment planning feedback to clients, as well as to ensure their full participation in choosing to move forward with treatment.

Before we give a description of the three treatment spheres, we would first like to present the dimensions included in our model (Table 5.1). Although we mentioned that these dimensions are similar to those of previous models, we have also added two dimensions that have not been the focus of other integrative models: (1) service-delivery context and (2) interprofessional collaboration. The service-delivery context dimension was added to better reflect the "real-life" service-delivery issues that clinician often need to face when providing services. Specifically, if you are working in a publicly funded clinic that has a limit of five sessions per client, you need to adapt your treatment plan accordingly. Although it would be wonderful to be able to provide as many individual client sessions as desired to clients, several contingencies preclude most therapeutic processes from allowing for this. As such, this model aims to be a viable option for a variety of contexts for service delivery. We believe that good clinicians advocate for their clients to ensure that they receive the services they need, and that often they can play an important role in this process by identifying the best strategies they can use given the resources allocated. In addition, when available, interprofessional collaboration should be encouraged and facilitated given the complexity of the real-life presentation of most clients. Too often, mental health providers and other health professionals develop treatment plans with limited knowledge of the goals and foci of other treatment providers; this is especially true when part of the services received are in the private sector and others in the public domain.

Table 5.1 displays the dimensions included in our model. A brief description of the elements included in each dimension is also found. Note that our description of these dimensions is greatly inspired and similar to the ones in Brook-Harris (2008) and Jones-Smith (2012), but we have supplemented some areas with relevant work by other authors (e.g., Kring and Sloan, 2010; APA, 1990). These descriptions are meant to provide a general idea of the elements included in each treatment spheres and are not meant to be exhaustive.

Table 5.1. Dimensions included in the Integrative Interprofessional Model for Treatment Planning and Monitoring

Thoughts	Automatic thoughts, assumptions, schemas, core beliefs, obsessions, intrusions, perceptions of self, others and the world.
Emotions	Emotions (triggers, attention, appraisal/goals, response), emotion regulation capacities, and distress tolerance capacities.
Behaviors	Behaviors that are maintaining current difficulties or helping maintain their well-being/coping styles (avoidance, distraction, overcompensation, compulsions, impulsivity, recklessness, assertiveness, participation in meaningful and productive activities, participation in pleasurable activities, socialization, isolation).
Biology and physical	Health, illnesses, other conditions that can affect psychological or physical well-being (for example, traumatic brain injury), disability, physiological activation, genetics, temperament, stigma associated with health or functional status, current and past treatments that could affect well-being, self-management of current illnesses, health habits.
Spirituality, religion, and existential issues	Views of healing, faith, life, death, and meaning creation.
Change process and preferences	Motivation to change, ambivalence, stages of change, perceived locus of control, expectations about change and treatment.
Interpersonal context	Closeness in relationships, ability to develop and maintain intimate relationships, ability to assert needs and boundaries, perceived social support, utilization of social support, conflicts, harassment, and abuse.
Service-delivery context	Resources available to treat the individual (financial, human /expertise, material). This can include, but is not limited to: number of sessions allotted, and professionals available.

Interprofessional collaboration	Professionals involved in the client's circle of care, current treatment received and by whom, referral process and consideration of inclusion of other professionals, consultation with other professionals.
Societal context	Political, socioeconomic and environmental factors, justice, stigma, and history.
Cultural context	Recognition of cultural diversity and sociocultural identification, acculturation, discrimination/bias/racism, immigration or refugee status, worldviews and views of self-influenced by culture, views of treatment based on culture, relevance of treatment and assessment strategies based on culture, generational conflicts, role of family members and community structures, expression of distress and taboos, fluency in the language of service-delivery.

Capacity and Self-Care—Filling the well, recharging the battery, and finding stability

This treatment sphere refers to the clients' ability to stabilize their symptoms and increase their coping with their current situation in a way that keeps them safe and maintains at minimum a basic level of functioning. It targets the clients' level of distress and emotion regulation skills at a more rudimentary level. For instance, an early treatment target may be their window of emotional tolerance (Siegel, 1999). When clients are above their window of tolerance or optimal arousal zone, they are "hyperaroused" and cannot integrate their emotional experience in a way that promotes a flexible and adaptive response (for example, extreme anxiety, flooded by emotions, and flashbacks). Conversely, when clients are under their window of tolerance, they are "hypoaroused" (for example, numb, confused, physical weakness) and cannot integrate the information coming from themselves or their environment because of lack of or insufficient arousal (see also Ogden, Minton, and Pain, 2006 or Brière, 2002). Therefore, if someone presents with major emotion dysregulation problems (for example, individuals who have been traumatized or suffer from a personality disorder, and/or severe anxiety/mood disorders), the therapist should focus on helping them safely modulate their level of arousal. Behaviors that are threatening the safety of the client and others would be of primary focus (e.g., suicidal or parasuicidal behaviors, impulsive behaviors, homicidal tendencies, substance abuse).

As part of this sphere, healthy life habits are also promoted, and risk factors are targeted (e.g., nutrition, exercise, sleep, smoking behaviors). Finally, it is within this sphere that we would highlight the strengths of the individual by identifying what are the resources (inner and external) already available to them (i.e., before treatment begins) that should be maintained or augmented.

Specific strategies that can be included at this level of treatment are: (1) behavioral (behavioral activation, minimizing avoidance where appropriate, response prevention of disruptive behaviors, self-monitoring, safety plans, and treatment/safety contracts when appropriate), (2) emotional (e.g., psychoeducation on emotions and experiential avoidance, introduction to emotion regulation exercises and strategies, self-compassion exercises, distress tolerance tools, self-soothing skills, and grounding techniques), (3) cognitive (e.g., psychoeducation to increase understanding of their symptoms, cognitive restructuring, problem-solving to increase safety and access resources, thought defusion, coping statements, and chain analysis), (4) biological (e.g., stabilizing sleep patterns, eating habits and level of physical activity, self-management of illnesses, inclusion of pharmaceutical strategies to help stabilize symptoms, relaxation and soothing with the five senses), (5) spiritual/religious/existential (e.g., creating meaning out of the experienced suffering and creating hope, using prayer or other spiritual rituals), (6) interpersonal (e.g., increasing socialization with safe individuals, assertiveness training, role-play/modeling), or (7) social (e.g., looking at housing issues, financial difficulties, access to care or other resources), and (8) cultural (e.g., addressing acculturation and discrimination issues).

The main goal is to empower the client to mobilize and become an active change agent in their life. Treatment strategies are aimed at helping client recognize that although their current patterns were helpful in the past, they now generate some suffering (i.e., to start to increase their awareness of the cost or pros of their current patterns/behaviors). For example, when working with a socially anxious individual, the therapist could suggest that: "considering what you have been through, it makes sense that you withdraw and isolate yourself when feeling criticized, at the same time I can see how lonely you feel and how much this interferes with your career goals." This is done in an empathic way to decrease shaming the client. Ambivalence, when present, is also explored (see Engle and Arkowitz,

2006 for an integrative approach in dealing with ambivalence in psychotherapy) because ambivalence toward change is always an important aspect
to consider during treatment. Remember that underlying these treatment
targets, like in all others, theoretical and empirical underpinnings (relational, evidence-based, strength-based, flexible, accountable, and interprofessional) are at play and should guide the choice of specific treatment
strategy in a client-centered approach.

Mastery and Competence of Self—Going beyond survival mode, sitting in the driving seat, being able to explore and create meaning

The goal of this treatment sphere is to help the client develop a more
integrated and positive sense of self and learn to develop more realistic
expectations and goals. It targets the ability of the client to make the
"implicit explicit." The more clients can start to increase their awareness
of their usually automatic or habitual response, the more they can slow
down the process and make better choices for themselves (i.e., action tendencies that are more in line with their life goals and values). Time is allocated to distill their experience, to help them make sense of their inner
world in a validating and empathic environment (see Elliott et al., 2004
for a good introduction to these concepts). Akin to the Capacity target,
links between thoughts, emotions, physical sensations, and behaviors are
made in light of the context clients needed to adapt to, but exploration
is deepened to go further than simply focusing on regulation and coping. In fact, research has shown that a certain level of emotional arousal
or experiencing is needed to promote change (Greenberg and Pascual-
Leone, 2006; Pascual-Leone and Greenberg, 2007). Ideally, clients have
now sufficient *distance* (see Gendlin, 1996) from their inner experience to
effectively work with it (i.e., they neither drown in it nor disown it). Painful experiences, inner dilemmas, or conflicts are highlighted, unpacked,
processed, and hopefully integrated or worked through in this treatment
sphere. The client's window of tolerance is also further expanded and reassessed. Clients can start to recognize their patterns in the context of
therapy but also in between sessions. Working hypotheses are derived and
tested (i.e., reality testing). Interventions are aimed at helping clients develop a higher sense of self-efficacy and mastery, and to contribute to a

more competent and sustainable sense of self that is better equipped to deal with future stressors and crises.

Specific strategies that can be used include: (1) behavioral (e.g., behavioral experiments, self-monitoring, in vivo exposure), (2) emotional (e.g., experiential exercises such as focusing, chair-work, imaginal confrontation, and exposure work), (3) cognitive (e.g., socratic questioning, cognitive restructuring of core beliefs, reframing, and mentalization), (4) spiritual/religious or existential (e.g., exploration of important life themes, meaning creation, building a coherent narrative), and (5) social (i.e., finding employment that aligns with their value and life goals, getting involved in advocacy or giving back to others). Special attention is given in helping client continue the work in between sessions (e.g., using home activities/practice/repetition) to promote consolidation and empowerment. A healthy balance between validation and stimulating change needs to be present within the therapeutic relationship. In fact, different approaches emphasize the need to find this equilibrium. For example, the main dialectic in dialectical behavioral therapy is acceptance and change (see Lynch, Chapman, Rosenthal, Kuo., and Linehan, 2006). In emotion-focused psychotherapy, relationship principles are paired with task principles, and clinicians are encouraged to be "standing on the edge of the client's experience" (Greenberg et al., 1993, p. 125). Said more succinctly, within this treatment sphere, the client needs to be encouraged to risk at a level that seems appropriate to them in the context of the safety of the therapeutic relationship to promote sustainable and meaningful change.

Mastery and Competence with Others—No one should have to drive alone. Connection, interdependence, authenticity, engagement and effectiveness

Although some level of interpersonal interventions are included in the other two treatment spheres, we believe that it is important to include a separate treatment sphere that focuses specifically on interpersonal functioning and effectiveness given the importance of interpersonal processes in shaping our views of self, others, and the world, and how we manage our emotions (see earlier section on relation/attachment). Perceived social support and secure attachment have been shown to be positive correlates of both physical and psychological health (see Greenman, Tassé, and Tulloch, 2015). In this treatment sphere, interpersonal situations (positive or conflictual) that occur outside of the therapy context are explored with curiosity to uncover potential dynamics of interest for therapeutic change. Strategies aimed at helping the client redefine their relationships to their environment are explored (e.g., renegotiating boundaries, seeking support from a more vulnerable stance). Issues related to grieving and loss would also be part of this treatment sphere. This sphere specifically targets cognitions, emotions, and behaviors that get in the way of creating meaningful relationships, negotiating conflicts, and asserting healthy boundaries. Another target for this sphere of treatment could include the exploration of manners by which a client could increase their sense of belonging to the community and to their culture, as well as their significant others. Although establishing a good relationship with the therapist is important, clinicians need to explore with their client on how they can recreate the safety of the therapeutic relationship with others outside of the therapeutic context. Special attention is also given to the "here and now" of the therapeutic relationship. Of importance, breaks in the alliance are explored and directly addressed to aim for a positive resolution. They are not seen as roadblocks but as an opportunity for the client and clinician to learn more about their collaboration, and for the client to practice important interpersonal skills that could be helpful outside of therapy.

Creating a Treatment Plan

First, it is important to understand that some interventions in one sphere of treatment can overlap with others. The three treatment spheres are not meant to be entirely mutually exclusive categories but as a general frame to help orient treatment, regardless of the theoretical orientation, the client's specific idiosyncrasies, the service context, and the particular clinician. What you should prioritize should be determined collaboratively with the client. Nevertheless, safety and stabilization issues (capacity) usually precede other types of interventions, especially with clients experiencing high level of distress or when the number of sessions is limited. In addition, monitoring treatment outcomes and developing a working alliance with clients will help to alert you to the possibility of your treatment plan requiring revisions or updates. This may appear abstract at this point. For this reason, the Chapter 6 will use the same clinical vignette used in Chapter 4 to help you better consolidate your understanding of our model and illustrate more concretely how to apply our model for service delivery. In the meantime, here is an example of how we could give feedback to the same client we met earlier, and how to discuss with him the treatment plan in a collaborative fashion based on this model.

Interview excerpt

Clinician: Mr. Scranton, I had the chance to review the information you provided in our last session, and I would like to propose a road map for our work together. While we do this together, it is important for me to know if you feel like my hypothesis about where you are at and what would be beneficial to work on makes sense to you. Does this fit for you?

Mr. Scranton: Sure.

C: First off, what struck me from our interview is how you have been "putting on your pants one leg at a time by yourself for over 50 years." What you have been able to achieve is quite remarkable.

Mr. S: Thanks. I always valued hard work and being independent.

C: That indeed seems very important to you, and this makes complete sense. Having a good work ethic is important for most of us, but also, it seems that through your life, being strong and responsible was important to you and your family.

Mr. S: Sure. Both my parents worked hard. I also had a lot of responsibilities.

C: Right. Would it be fair to say that these experiences help shape this view of yourself as this independent strong man that needs to take care of others?

Mr. S: Yes.

C: Can you tell me more about this?

Mr. S: Well, I always feel like I need to take care of everyone and provide you know. That is what a man is supposed to do.

C: Right. Be strong. Provide. Work hard. That is really important to how you see yourself.

Mr. S: Yes . . . yes.

C: What comes to mind for me is: here was this man working hard, providing, being strong, looking forward to retirement, and then illness struck. An illness that confronted this view of himself as this self-sufficient man and kind of "took things away from you" as you mentioned in our last session . . . it made you feel . . .

Mr. S: Weak, dependent

C: More vulnerable, right?

Mr. S: Yes (starts to tear up), but that's life. Don't want to talk about it.

C: Huhmm . . . I get that. These things are very difficult to talk about, especially if this part of you, the more vulnerable part, has not been given a lot of space in your life.

Mr. S: What do you mean?

C: We all have a more vulnerable part. I know I have it too. However, for most of us, we learned to tuck this away, not talk about it, or avoid it. This seems to work for a while, but then, when we go through very difficult situations, like your heart attack, we can't avoid it any longer. It is there, demanding attention. For most of us, it is hard to know what to do with it.

Mr. S: Yes. I learned that men should not cry. Crying is weak. Pathetic really.

C: Yes, you learned that this part of you is not "okay," and you seem to be working really hard at keeping it inside.

Mr. S: I want to forget about it . . .

C: Right. Forget about it. Push it away. At the same time, it seems that it never really goes away does it?

Mr. S: no . . . sometimes it get[s] worse . . .

C: Yes. That is the downfall of pushing it away. I tend to say that emotions are like water boiling in a pot on the stove, if you put a lid on boiling water, for a while it seems fine, but then . . .

Mr. S: It explodes.

C: Exactly. You have been harboring a lot of feelings relating to the consequences of your heart attack. All the changes. The losses.

Mr. S: Yes, but I don't know what to do with it. All I do is get angry at myself, my wife, the world. I try to keep my mind off of it or stay home . . .

C: You try to shut down. You don't ask for help, try to deal on your own or withdraw.

Mr. S: Yes, exactly . . . but nothing really works. . . .

C: Would you like some help with this?

Mr. S: Yes . . . but I really don't know what you can do.

C: Here is what I have been thinking about. I usually look at three targets for my work with clients: Capacity and Self-care, Mastery and Competence with Self, and Mastery and Competence with Others (the clinician draws three circle on a sheet of paper in front of Mr. S:). In the capacity target, we look at things that you might need to help recharge and find stability following the heart attack or for other reasons. For example, in your case, it could be looking at ways to reduce your panic attacks, decrease your sleep difficulties, increase your energy levels and interest in pleasurable activities, and decrease your outbursts.

Mr. S: This would be nice . . . what would that look like?

C: Well, for panic attacks, specific treatment plans have been developed that are shown to be quite effective. They usually entail identifying your thoughts, feelings, and behaviors in regards to these attacks and try to challenge thoughts that lead to more anxiety and panic. Part of the treatment plan is also to help increase your tolerance to some physical sensations that you currently see as dangerous through what we call exposure work. Of course, I would detail all of this in each session for you to make sure that this still fits with what you want to work on. I realize that words such as exposure might be a bit vague right now.

Mr. S: Okay. . . .

C: In the Capacity sphere, we also look at ways to maintain healthy life habits, as they tend to have an impact on our mood. For example, we know that exercising can help with depressive symptoms and that drinking too much alcohol can decrease our mood. Having a healthy and balance[d] diet is also important. However, I wanted to gauge with you what you think about changing these habits?

Mr. S: Well, I know I have to exercise more and eat better. I should also quit smoking and drinking, but I just feel like it's a lot to change at one time.

C: Of course, it must feel a bit overwhelming to have to change of all of this at once.

Mr. S: Yes, it does. I like eating steak and fries and drinking beer . . .

C: I get that! I like it too. It would be hard for me, or anyone, to let go of the things we like. At the same time, I see that a part of you is worried about having another heart attack. It's like a part of you wants to maintain these life habits because they bring something for you (pleasure, calm), but another part is scared of where they could lead. Does this fit?

Mr. S: Totally. It's like an internal tug of war. I know I should change, but part of me does not want to.

C: Hum hum. Well, maybe we could start there? We could look at these two parts. It's what we call ambivalence. Once we understand more about the wants/needs of these two parts, then we could get a better sense of what you want to start changing and slowly start to make changes. Would that work?

Mr. S: Yes . . . it would feel more manageable.

C: We could also look at who we could include in our collaboration to help with some of those changes to increase the level of support you are receiving. For example, we could talk to the nurse, dietician, or kinesiologist? Does this seem like something that you would be open to?

Mr. S: Yes . . . but later down the road . . .

C: Okay. Let's just stay with the two parts for now and then reassess the inclusion of other health professional down the road.

C: In the Capacity sphere, we also look at quick changes that we can make that could have the "biggest bang for our buck" or as I like to say, bigger changes with minimal efforts (laughs). When I looked at your situation, it became clear to me that how you are currently using your medication could be contributing to some of your difficulties. For example, we know from research that antidepressants need to be taken on a daily basis versus when we want to get the maximum effect. Your Nitroglycerin use also does not seem optimal.

Mr. S: I did not know that.

C: Yes. And that's why I thought that it could be a good idea for you to talk to Dr. Sobel and get more information on your medication to make sure that the way you are using them is in line with the other work that we are going to do.

Mr. S: Okay, I can do this.

C: Also, I find it important to rule out any physical conditions that could potentially be contributing to your current difficulties. Upon reviewing the information I gathered during our intake session, it sounds to me that some symptoms you are experiencing: your frequent awakenings, breathing pauses, restless nights could be linked to obstructive sleep apnea. This condition has also been associated with depression. Therefore, if this fits for you, I would highly recommend that we talk to Dr. Sobel to recommend a sleep assessment as there could be potential treatments to help with this, which are outside of the scope of my competencies.

Mr. S: I did not know that. I thought that it was just how I sleep. Ok, you can recommend this to Dr. Sobel.

C: And you also mentioned something really important in our last session. It seems that a lot of the things you are doing—smoking, drinking—is to help with making you deal with emotions and stress. Does that fit?

Mr. S: Yes.

C: I was wondering if we could introduce new ways of dealing with stress and your emotions, then maybe these behaviors would not be as needed.

Mr. S: Makes sense.

C: Therefore, while we work on your ambivalence to make these changes, we could start to introduce new ways of coping and dealing with your current situation to build you capacity, which will help us down the road once you start to make some changes.

Mr. S: Sounds good.

C: Do you have any questions about the elements included in the Capacity target?

Mr. S: No, sounds like a plan to me.

C: Okay. Now, we can also look at what we could do in the Mastery and Competence of Self target. Here, we want to go beyond survival mode. The image I have is the following: currently you are drowning and need to find a way to keep your head above water

(Capacity), but living a life where you are only surviving is also quite tiring, wouldn't you say?

Mr. S: Completely.

C: The Mastery and Competence of Self helps you become a better swimmer so that it feels you can enjoy being in the water. It also helps build a boat that you can go in and go explore the world even if you had a heart attack. Does this make sense?

Mr. S: Yes . . . but how?

C: Good question. First off, we can look at how some ways that you think about yourself, the world, others, and your emotions (or vulnerable side) can create unnecessary pain. Life is painful for all of us, but sometimes we add to that suffering by putting too much pressure on ourselves, and having rules about how we should be and behave. Often these have been learned from our family, society, or culture, and they can be helpful on some occasions, but when we apply these rules with rigidity, not a lot of flexibility, they can leave us feeling quite depressed and anxious. For example, if you learned that a man should not cry because this is weak, then it can make it difficult to grieve the understandable sadness that comes from the loss related to the heart attack.

Mr. S: Don't know if I like the sound of that (laughs), but I get it.

C: Does it seem a bit foreign for you to be asked to look within yourself?

Mr. S: Not a bit foreign, but completely new.

C: Right. And I don't know about you, but for most, what is "new" can also be a bit scary. Does that fit?

Mr. S: Yes, what if I don't like what I find? What if I fall apart?

C: Right. A part of you is scared of what it means to go inward. Will you lose yourself? Will it become overwhelming? These are frequent fears, and it makes complete sense. Let me reassure you, however, that the goal is not to make you lose yourself, but help you access a part of yourself that you tend to hide/tuck away. The goal here is not to go all-at-once, open the door completely, but to slowly and with curiosity start to expand your awareness of you as a whole. You set the pace. To go back to the swimming analogy, the goal is not to push you in the deep end, but to help you dip your toes, so that you can gradually go further and further into the water.

Mr. S: Hum. I am willing to give it a try.

C: We can always reassess your openness to this. Today the goal is to provide you with options to help deal with your current difficulties.

Mr. S: Like a menu of options.

C: Exactly. I offer, you pick!

Mr. S: What about the Mastery and Competence with Others?

C: Well, this target includes some things related to the other two, put I decided to make a different target because we know from research how important it is for human beings to feel like they belong, that they are a part of something, that we are not on our own. We are social mammals after all. Relationships are really important for both our mental and physical health. For example, perceived social isolation has been found to be a predictor for mortality caused by cardiovascular disease. Also, patients who are married are more likely to be alive 15 years after a heart bypass than unmarried patients.

Mr. S: Really? I guess that in this sphere, we could work on the problems I have with my wife and my colleagues.

C: Exactly. We would look at what are the challenges related to "being with" others in a way that is satisfying for both you and others. For example, we would look at what blocks you from getting support from others, or what are your triggers in relationship that leads to conflict.

Mr. S: Oh. . . . I have a lot of triggers (laughs).

C: Sounds like it (laughs). We can also invite your wife for a session if needed or make a referral to marriage counseling should we find that this would be useful. One thing that I want to make space for in our discussion today is also your sexual intimacy. I understand that for most people, talking about this leads to feeling embarrassed or ashamed. However, sexuality is a natural part of our experience and relationships. Unfortunately, when we have a physical illness, sometimes the illness itself or the medication relating to it can have an impact on our ability to engage in sexual activities in the way that we used to. Many of my clients report erectile difficulties or changes in their desire. Often, they feel too ashamed to talk about it. What saddens me about this is that they suffer in silence when often there are remedies or ways to improve their sexuality.

Mr. S: Really?

C: Yes. Your physician, for example, would be quite knowledgeable in helping you with this.

Mr. S: Not sure I feel ready to talk about it with Dr. Sobel.

C: That's okay, but would you like us, at one point in time, to look at how you could start the conversation with Dr. Sobel?

Mr. S: Okay.

C: So as you can see, we can focus on Capacity (stabilizing/keeping your head above water), Mastery and Competence of Self (slowly start to get out of survival mode to lead a more satisfying life), and Mastery and Competence with Others (feeling like we belong, part of, supported) to help you cope with the aftermath of your heart attack. This being said, I would like to point out that in all three spheres, I found that you already had strengths and resources. Without even doing any treatment, you are already implementing things that are helpful. For example, you told me that, on occasions, you do go and seek out the support of your friends. You also care deeply about your wife and your family. You noted that a part of you is already aware of some of the changes that you need to make to live a healthier lifestyle. These are all important. And while you told me that you don't know what to do with your emotions, what I have noticed is that, even if it's uncomfortable, you have the courage to access them, dip your toe.

Mr. S: Hum . . . this makes me feel uncomfortable . . . but a good kind of uncomfortable.

C: (Laughs). So where would you like us to start our work?

Mr. S: Well, I want to really stop the panic attacks and better manage my anger. So the Capacity target seems the most appropriate.

C: Okay. This is actually a great plan. Usually, we do start with the Capacity target. Note however, that we will reevaluate on a frequent basis if this is still the target you want to focus on, or should we shift to something else. Often, we can focus on more than one at once.

Mr. S: Okay, sounds good to me.

C: Before we leave, can I ask how you felt about today's session?

Mr. S: I got more out of it than I thought.

C: Is there anything that you would have like to be different or that you did not like?

Mr. S: Well, I like it when you give me images. It helps. I need more of that.

C: Okay, sounds good. I will try to include more images on paper. So let's start next session with the Capacity target and working on your panic attacks.

Mr. S: Great, see you next week.

References

American Psychological Association. (1990). *Guidelines for providers of psychological services to ethnic, linguistic, and culturally, diverse populations*. Washington, DC: Author. Retrieved from: http://www.apa.org /pi/oema/resources/policy/provider-guidelines.aspx

Bowlby, J. (1969). *Attachment and loss. vol. 1: Attachment* (2nd ed.). New York: Basic Books.

Bowlby, J. (1988). *A secure base: Parent and child attachment and healthy human development*. New York: Basic Books.

Brière, J. (2002). Treating adult survivors of severe childhood abuse and neglect : Further development of an integrative model. In J.E.B. Myers, L. Berliner, J. Briere, C.T. Hendrix, T. Reid, and C. Jenny (Eds.) *The APSAC handbook on child maltreatment* (2 nd Ed.) (pp. 175-202). Newbury Park, CA: Sage Publications.

Brooks-Harris, J. E. (2008). *Integrative multitheoretical psychotherapy*. Boston: Houghton Mifflin.

Cassidy, J., and Shaver, P.R. (2008). Handbook of attachment : Theory, research, and clinical applications (2nd ed.). New York: Guildford Press.

Costello, P. C. (2013). *Attachment-based psychotherapy : Helping patients develop adaptive capacities*. Washington, DC : American Psychological Association.

Elliott, R., Watson, J. C., Goldman, R. N., and Greenberg, L. S. (2004). *Learning emotion-focused therapy: The process-experiential approach to change*. Washington, DC: American Psychological Association.

Engle, D., and Arkowitz, Hal. (2006). *Ambivalence in psychotherapy: Facilitating readiness to change*. New York: Guilford Press.

Gendlin, E.T. (1996). *Focusing-oriented psychotherapy: A manual of the experiential method*. New York: Guilford.

Greenberg, L. S., Rice, L. N., and Elliott, R. (1993). *Facilitating emotional change: the moment-by-moment process*. New York: Guildford Press.

Greenberg, L. S., and Pascual-Leone, A. (2006). Emotion in psychotherapy: A practice-friendly research review. *Journal Of Clinical Psychology, 62(5)*, 611-630. doi:10.1002/jclp.20252.

Greenman, P. S., Tassé, V., and Tulloch, H. (2015). Straight to the heart: Romantic relationships, attachment, and the management of cardiac disease. In A. Rennolds. (Ed). *Psychology of interpersonal perception and relationships*, (pp. 157-174). New York: Nova Science Publishers Inc.

Holm-Hadulla, R. M., Hofmann, F., and Sperth, M. (2011). An integrative model of counseling. *Asia Pacific Journal of Counselling and Psychotherapy, 2*(1), 3-24. doi:10.1080/21507686.2010.546864.

Jones-Smith, E. (2012). Integrative psychotherapy : constructing your own Integrative approach to therapy. In E. Jones-Smith. Theories of counseling and psychotherapy: An integrative approach (pp. 585-611). Los Angeles: SAGE Publications Inc. Retrieved from: http://www.sisdca.it/public/pdf/Integrative-Psychotherapy.pdf

Johnson, S. M. (2009). Attachment theory and emotionally focused therapy for individuals and couples: Perfect partners. In J. H. Obegi and E. Berant. (Eds.). Attachment theory and research in clinical work in adults. New York: Guildford Press.

Kring, A., and Sloan, Denise M. (Eds.), (2010). *Emotion regulation and psychopathology: A transdiagnostic approach to etiology and treatment*. New York, NY: Guilford Press.

Lambert, M. J. (2013). Outcome in psychotherapy: The past and important advances. *Psychotherapy, 50*(1), 42-51. doi:10.1037/a0030682.

Lecompte, C., Savard, R., Drouin, M-S., and Guillon, V. (2004). Qui sont les psychothérapeutes efficacies? Implications pour la formation en psychologie. *Revue québécoise de psychologie, 25(3)*, 73-102

Lynch, T. R., Chapman, A. L., Rosenthal, M. Z., Kuo, J. R., and Linehan, M. M. (2006). Mechanisms of change in dialectical behavior therapy: Theoretical and empirical observations. *Journal of Clinical Psychology, 62(4),* 459-480.

Miller, S. D., Hubble, M. and Duncan, B. (2008). The secrets of supershrinks: Pathways to clinical excellence. *Psychotherapy Networker,* 3-10. Retrieved from: http://www.scottdmiller.com/wp-content/uploads/2014/06/Supershrinks-Free-Report-1.pdf.

Ogden, P., Minton, K., and Pain, C. (2006). *Trauma and the body: A sensorimotor approach to psychotherapy.* New York: Norton.

Pascual-Leone, A., Greenberg, L. S., (2007). Emotional processing in experiential therapy: Why "the only way out is through". *Journal of Consulting and Clinical Psychology, 75*(6), 875-887. doi:10.1037/0022-006X.75.6.875

Prochaska, J. O., and DiClemente, C. C. (1984). *The transtheoretical approach : Crossing the traditional boundaries of therapy.* Homewood, IL : Dow-Jones/Irwin.

Prochaska, J. O., and DiClemente, C. C. (2005). The transtheoretical approach. In J. C. Norcross and M. R. Goldfried (Eds.), *Handbook of psychotherapy integration* (2nd ed.)., (pp. 147-171) . New York: Oxford University Press.

Rogers, C. R. (1961). *On becoming a person.* Boston: Houghton Mifflin.

Rogers, C. R. (1992). The necessary and sufficient conditions of therapeutic personality change. *Journal of Consulting and Clinical Psychology, 60*(6), 0827-832. doi:10.1037/0022-006X.60.6.827

Siegel, D.J. (1999). *The developing mind: How relationships and the brain interact to shape who we are.* New York; Guilford Press.

Skovholt, T., and Jennings, Len. (2004). *Master therapists: Exploring expertise in therapy and counseling.* Boston: Pearson/Allyn and Bacon.

Walfish, S., McAlister, B., O'Donnell, P., and Lambert, M. J. (2012). An investigation of self-assessment bias in mental health providers. *Psychological Reports, 110(2),* 639–644. doi:10.2466/02.07.17.PR0.110.2.639- 644.

Wampold, B. E., and Imel, Z. E. (2015). *The great psychotherapy debate: the evidence for what makes psychotherapy work (2nd edition).* New York: Taylor and Francis Inc.

Wylie, M. S., and Turner, L. (2011). The attuned therapist : Does attachment theory really matter? *Psychotherapy Networker, 35(2),* 1-10.

CHAPTER 6

Treatment Delivery and Monitoring

A Short Vignette

In Chapter 5, we introduced our Integrative Interprofessional Model for Psychological Treatment, which revolved around three treatment spheres: Capacity and Self-care, Mastery and Competence of Self, and Mastery and Competence with Others. Using the same case vignette, we will attempt to illustrate more explicitly how this model can be useful for treatment delivery and monitoring. The basic information and initial impressions of the referral agent will not be repeated. We present here an example on when the clinician has to adjust their treatment plan based on treatment progress and client preferences. The aim is to illustrate how the framework provides the flexibility to tailor the interventions to the needs of the client without losing track of the broader conceptualization. It also depicts the importance of monitoring and checking in with clients to ensure that the interventions are meaningful and relevant to their experience, further fostering a culture of collaboration and feedback.

Clinical Case Vignette

Clinician: At our last session, we agreed to focus on the Capacity sphere, and take a closer look at your panic attacks (the clinician takes out the drawing of the three treatment spheres developed with the client during last session). Does this still fit with what you wanted to work on today?

Mr. Scranton: Well, I do want to work on this, but I think we should focus on something more pressing.

C: Okay. Can you tell me more about it?

Mr. S.: Well. I feel bad about it. I was scheduled for an appointment with Dr. Sobel yesterday but I cancelled.

C: Was it an appointment that you had made or a routine appointment?

Mr. S.: It was a routine appointment. I was supposed to go see him to follow up on my blood work and medication.

C: I am glad that you are sharing this with me. Would you like us to explore what happened?

Mr. S.: Oh, I know what happened. I did not want to go, because I didn't want to face the fact that I haven't implemented the changes he has recommended. Last time I saw him, he noted that I should lose 20 pounds and start exercising more regularly. He said I needed to change my diet. As you know. I have done none of those things. So what's the point in going to see him?

C: If you haven't made the prescribed changes, it's not worth it to go see him.

Mr. S.: Exactly.

C: At the same time, it seems that a part of you is not comfortable with this situation?

Mr. S.: Well, Dr. Sobel is nice. I hate to cancel on him. I just didn't want to go.

C: Can you tell me more about this part that just "didn't want to go"?

Mr. S.: I felt like a fool. I did not want him to be mad at me or tell me that he does not want to be my doctor anymore because I am not taking his recommendations seriously.

C: Hum. So as you imagined yourself going to your appointment with Dr. Sobel, you imagined him getting mad at you, not wanting to treat you anymore because you hadn't made the changes he asked.

Mr. S.: Yes, all these worries were going through my head.

C: And what was going on inside of you, in your body as you imagined going there?

Mr. S.: I felt a pressure in my chest, tightness.

C: Can you feel this right now as we are talking about it?

Mr. S.: Yes, but I don't like feeling this way.

C: There is this pressure in your chest, tightness, and when you feel this, it sounds like a part of you says, avoid this, don't go there, don't stay with these unpleasant sensations. Does this fit?

Mr. S.: Oh yes, I can't wait for you to change the topic of conversation (laughs).

C: (Laughs). Right. Somehow, focusing your attention on what you are feeling in this moment is uncomfortable.

Mr. S.: I really don't like it.

C: You really don't like it. Does this happen often, when you feel this pressure in your chest, or tightness, or even when you feel bad, that you just want to avoid these sensations or feelings?

Mr. S.: Oh yes.

C: There is something really uncomfortable about feeling bad, feeling the pressure in your chest, and somehow it feels better to just run away from these sensations and feelings right?

Mr. S.: Yes. That's it.

C: And once you avoid these feelings or sensations, how do you feel?

Mr. S.: I feel relieved.

C: Considering what you just said, could it be what happened with your appointment? You did not want to feel bad, so it felt better to cancel, avoid seeing Dr. Sobel?

Mr. S.: Exactly. When I cancelled, I felt relieved. Like, I dodged a bullet.

C: Initially, there was a sense of relief. Would you say that you felt calmer? Less anxious?

Mr. S.: Yes, I did not have to worry about what he would say, I could just forget about it.

C: That makes sense. Most often when people feel anxious, they want to avoid feeling this way; therefore, they stop doing whatever brings their anxiety to the forefront. For example, if it makes them anxious to engage in public speaking, then they don't sign up for oral presentations at work. If they worry about having a conversation with their wife because it will lead to a conflict, then they withdraw and shutdown. It makes sense. We tend to want to avoid what makes us uncomfortable. On the other hand, there is usually a downfall to this.

Mr. S.: Like what? Sounds good to me.

C: Well, we never get a chance to see if what we fear really does come true, and we limit ourselves. Here is an example: if you had a little boy come to you screaming because he believed there was a monster under his bed, what would you do?

Mr. S.: I would go check under the bed with him to show him that there is no monster.

C: Right. You wouldn't tell him to run away, go sleep in another room, or distract himself until he falls asleep?

Mr. S.: No. That would be stupid.

C: Why is that?

Mr. S.: Well, he would never learn that there is no monster under his bed.

C: Right. He would never learn that what he was really worried about might not actually happen. What else? What happens if he goes to sleep in another room and then thinks that there is a monster under this new bed, and the next, and the next, but he never verifies this . . .

Mr. S.: He will have to start sleeping on the floor!

C: Laughs. Right, his life would become less and less comfortable, and he would be running out of options. There would a big cost. Sleeping on the floor each night, being afraid every night before going to bed, for something that might not even be true.

Mr. S.: Okay, I see where you are going with this. If I always avoid, there is a cost in the long run.

C: Most often there is. If we apply it to your current situation: not going to see Dr. Sobel, were there costs or negative consequences for you?

Mr. S.: I didn't get to find out the results of my blood work to see if things have improved or not. I didn't get to see if my medication is working or not.

C: And how does this "not knowing" make you feel?

Mr. S.: Not good. I would like to know.

C: It would be important to know, wouldn't it? Are there other costs? After you cancelled and you felt relief, what happened next inside of you?

Mr. S.: Well, I started to feel guilty, I don't like cancelling appointments. I am also afraid of booking a next appointment. What will Dr. Sobel say then?

C: Hm hm. So while there was this initial relief, other feelings emerged soon after, like guilt, fear. Your brain also started to worry about the next appointments and how Dr. Sobel would view you.

Mr. S.: And I did not get a chance to get my results. So yes, the trade-off does not seem worth it, does it?

C: There seems to be more cost for you to cancel than to attend.

Mr. S.: Yes, but I really don't like it that I have not made the suggested changes.

C: I hear you. While you see that there is more cost in cancelling, it does not change the part of you that is really scared of going to see him and face him.

Mr. S.: I just feel like I am failing. Why go there, if he is going to tell me that I am a failure? I already feel like it. I don't need any reminders.

C: Hum. Sounds like a part of you is really harsh about all of this. When you look at how difficult it has been to implement the changes, a part of you tells you that you are a failure, not only in your own eyes, but also in the eyes of Dr. Sobel. That must be tough.

Mr. S.: It does not feel good.

C: Can you tell me more about what it feels like when a part of you says you are a failure?

Mr. S.: Well, this is where I get the tightness in my chest, and I want to run away. I hate this feeling. It makes me feel small.

C: Makes you feel small. So when you imagine yourself going to see Dr. Sobel, it's like a part of you says, beware, you are going to get into trouble, you have not worked hard enough, you are a failure, and that makes you feel small and ashamed. And when you reached that place, you don't want to stay with these uncomfortable feelings, the best available option is to avoid, to run away. And while running away offers some initial relief, it does not help the part of you that is really concerned for your health.

Mr. S.: (The client is silent for a while). I am trying you know, I really want to stay alive and be in my family's life for a long time, it's just so hard.

C: Of course. You have had to adjust to a lot. And right now, when you realize that you have not made the suggested changes, it sounds like a part of you is really hard on you. Beats you down.

Mr. S.: Yes. That's what it feels like. Like I am beating myself up. But I have always done that.

C: You have always been hard on yourself?

Mr. S.: Yes. I always had to achieve, perform, and be the best. Failure was never an option.

C: And right now, you are struggling, and instead of having a compassionate part of you that takes care of you and helps you, you have this part telling you are failing.

Mr. S.: I have always learned that the best way is to kick yourself in the butt.

C: Right, that's what you've learned. Kick yourself in the butt. But it sounds like right now, this way of treating yourself is not really helping you.

Mr. S.: No, it's making things worse. I just don't know how to do it any other way.

C: Let's see if we can try to change this a little. While we can work on helping you be kinder and more compassionate towards yourself, let's start by challenging this belief that Dr. Sobel will think you are a failure because you haven't made the required changes. It seems that this could be a good place to start. Maybe we could experiment there.

Mr. S.: I already know that he would not say this. He is kind. I know it. It's more me. I feel like that.

C: What do you think Dr. Sobel would say if he were to know that you cancelled because you felt bad and you were afraid of having failed in his eyes?

Mr. S.: Well, he would say that it is too bad, because he wants to help me.

C: Right, he wants what is best for you. Do you think that he understands how hard it is to make the changes he is recommending?

Mr. S.: I guess. I might not be the first one that has a hard time with losing weight or changing my diet or to quit smoking.

C: I agree. I always say that if making changes were that easy, I would not have a job (laughs).

Mr. S.: Laughs. I guess making changes can be difficult.

C: Of course, and it is even harder when a part of you is telling you that we are failing. That is really depleting.

Mr. S.: Yes, it does. It makes you want to hide and forget all about it.

C: Exactly. When you start to be hard on yourself, it hurts, it makes you feel small, and it feels like the only place to go is to hide and run away. While this offers short-term relief, it also comes at a cost.

Mr. S.: I guess I should go to this appointment.

C: What would you need to help you go?

Mr. S.: I guess that I just have to remind myself that I am not the only one struggling with this and that Dr. Sobel has seen other people like me, and he still continues to help them.

C: Sounds like a good plan. Let's see this as an experiment. Like the boy who took the risk to look under his bed. Let's use your appointment with Dr. Sobel as a way to gather more information about you. Maybe you could try to pay attention to what goes on in your body, your mind, and what you are feeling before, during, and after your appointment with Dr. Sobel. Does this seem feasible?

Mr. S.: Yes.

C: Here is a sheet of paper highlighting the important things to watch for before, during, and after your appointment (gives client a three-column sheet of paper with the headers before, during, and after, and in each column there is a specific place to right thoughts—perceptions, emotions, body sensations, and urges).

C: It can also be interesting to look at if your predictions came true or not (e.g., Was Dr. Sobel really mad? Did he say he wanted to stop treating you?). All this information you will be gathering is really important for our work in session. Please bring back this sheet to our next appointment, and we can look at it together. Would this work for you?

Mr. S.: Yes. This could work. If it goes badly, you will be the first to hear about it (laughs).

C: I am counting on it. I will be right here.

In this excerpt, we illustrate the importance of always checking in with clients to see if what you had planned to work on during the session is in accordance with their own goals. Most often, novel clinicians are reticent at the idea of allowing this flexibility to occur. We believe that our three treatment spheres can be helpful in calming your anxiety of "not following the plan." Each treatment sphere allows the flexibility to focus on what is more relevant to the client at the moment. Here, Mr. Scranton is discussing his worries and shame about cancelling his appointment with Dr. Sobel. This is a rich situation because it most likely taps into his core view of self, others, and the world as well as his coping and usual emotional regulation strategies. This vignette illustrated integrative treatment interventions aimed at all three spheres, with the primary goal being to start to help Mr. Scranton organize his experience by seeing the interrelation between his thoughts, emotions, physical sensations, and behaviors. The clinician was also helping Mr. Scranton examine the cost-benefit of maintaining his current way of coping (avoidance) (sphere 1) and exploring with him new ways to manage the situation that would help him get his needs met and feel more competent in managing the important parts of his life (sphere 2) and within relationships (sphere 3).

Of importance, in this excerpt, we illustrate the importance for the clinician to maintain a stance of curiosity versus shaming the client for cancelling his appointment. Psychoeducation was given in a way that was normalizing and related to Mr. Scranton's experience. Instead of taking on the role of a teacher who is *telling* his pupil about the link between avoidance and anxiety, the clinician was collaboratively engaging Mr. Scranton. Images and metaphors can often be useful tools to convey important concepts in a way that remains meaningful to clients. The clinician was also using Mr. Scranton's words. By staying as close as possible to Mr. Scranton's experience, the clinician is helping Mr. Scranton connect with his inner world. The clinician is slowly shifting the focus inward in a nonjudgmental way to gradually help Mr. Scranton connect and tolerate "being with" his emotions and start to improve his emotion regulation capacities. By providing a flexible approach and allowing Mr. Scranton to have the space to discuss what was pressing for him (his preference), the clinician is also working on building the alliance, which will hopefully translate into Mr. Scranton being more invested in the treatment process.

Finally, please keep in mind that the excerpt presented in this chapter is only an example of how to work within the various treatment spheres. The specific techniques or language used can vary from one provider to the other depending on their theoretical orientations, characteristics, and their client's idiosyncrasies. Chapter 7 will provide you with another example to further illustrate the use of our framework when the clinician is pressed for time.

CHAPTER 7

Conducting an Intake and Treatment Planning Session

We have presented both the rationale behind our integrative and inter-professional model for assessment and treatment planning, and we have applied it to a clinical vignette. In this chapter, we present the full transcript of an intake session with a private practice client, to show how this model can be used within the context of a single assessment and treatment planning session. Too often, because of the high volumes of patients and fast-pace environment of most mental health services, clinicians cannot dedicate multiple sessions to assessment, feedback, and agreement on treatment plan. To remain relevant and useful, clinicians need to be able to use appointment time efficiently by: (1) quickly assessing the presenting problems; (2) swiftly identify the treatment spheres to target; and (3) competently summarize their findings to the patient in order to collaboratively plan treatment. As such, we wish to illustrate how our model can be adjusted to meet the needs and realities of various contexts of practice.

Lydia is a 28-year-old Asian American government employee. She contacted the clinician and requested an appointment as soon as possible to address what she called "significant problems." After revealing that she had just been put on sick leave, she said that she was happy to take any appointment time, as long as it was soon. Lydia arrives early for her intake appointment a few days later. She sits in the waiting room, staring at the floor, wringing her hands. When the clinician approaches her, she instantly perks up and offers a shy smile. He gives her information to review including his policy on informed consent and limits of confidentiality, as well as an identification form to complete for her file, and two short self-reported measures to assess current depressive and anxious symptomatology, as well as a general measure of psychological distress that is commonly used to both assess initial symptomatology as well as monitor treatment outcome. She readily complies with the task. When he returns a few minutes later to see how things are coming along, she hands them back to him, fully completed. Lydia follows him to his office, where he quickly scores both short scales to find that she is reporting severe depressive symptomatology and moderate anxiety. These findings are consistent with her results on the measure of general distress, which also suggests that she suffers from poor social support. Notably, she did not endorse any of the "critical items" related to suicidal and homicidal risk. After having reviewed the limits of confidentiality and obtained informed consent, he begins the assessment process targeting the six areas of inquiry described in Chapter 3.

> **Clinician:** Hi Lydia, you mentioned that you were struggling with significant issues when we spoke briefly on the phone. Perhaps, we can start by you telling me a bit more about what has been going on for you?
>
> **Lydia:** Yeah, sure. Hmm, yeah significant problems. My doctor put me on a 2-week sick leave just a few days ago. I didn't think that it was necessary, but now . . . . (trails off, looks out the window as her eyes well up) . . . I don't know . . . (she hides her face in her hands as she starts to weep softly).
>
> **C:** It sounds like it's been a really difficult time. (Lydia nods as she tried to compose herself). Let's just take it one thing at a time. What made you decide to go see your doctor? *[Focuses on presenting symptoms and slowing down the process to help the client remain within an appropriate window of tolerance to avoid dysregulation].*
>
> **L:** I was feeling really tired all the time, like I couldn't concentrate. I would just stare at the computer screen at work and not get anything done. I'm sure everybody thinks I'm such a loser.
>
> **C:** When did this start? *[Remains focused on symptoms with the intent of clarifying the nature, duration, and intensity of symptomatology, but also takes note of the self-critical statement Lydia made for follow-up later].*

L: This time? Well I guess it started after I got this, hmm, I guess you'd call it a promotion. *[Takes note of the possibility that there have been previous depressive/anxious episodes].*

C: Tell me about this "promotion."

L: Yeah, okay. So they have this program at work where if your manager feels that you, I don't know, are like pretty good at your job and you perform well consistently enough, then they can recommend you for this program that can fast-track your promotion to a higher rank. I really don't know why my manager thought I would qualify for this, but anyways he recommended me about a year ago, and then a few months back at my performance evaluation, he told me I was accepted in the program and that I was getting a promotion (Lydia hangs her head appearing dejected).

C: That sounds like good news, but you don't seem happy at all as you're telling me about it. Can you help me understand?

L: I just knew from the moment he said that I got it that it was only a matter of time until they all found out how big of a fraud I am.

C: A fraud? In what way? *[Shows genuine curiosity using a soft tone of voice to help develop a sense of safety in the working alliance].*

L: I am nothing special. I don't deserve special treatment. Things just come easy to me. It's not like I worked for it . . . It's just not fair (Lydia's voice turns to a whisper as she mouths the last words).

C: Okay, so after you received this promotion, you began to feel more tired, less energized? And you noticed that it was becoming more difficult to do your work? Is that it?

L: Yes, exactly. I would sleep all night, but I wouldn't feel like getting up in the morning even though I probably slept like nine or ten hours. I usually go to the gym a few times per week to help with my energy levels, but even that isn't working anymore. I would get to work and sometimes I'd realize I had been staring at my inbox for half an hour and done nothing. Then I would try to read something, and I would read it and reread it and still it's like I never read it in the first place.

C: Did you find any other changes in your mood or your habits?

L: Yeah, I don't feel like doing anything anymore. I'm just a big lazy potato. I get home and I just stare at the wall. Literally. Can you believe that?

C: Yes, actually, and it sounds like this is very upsetting.

L: Yes, I mean, I was never the life of the party, but now I don't feel like doing anything. I don't go out because I don't read anything, and everybody is just so on top of things. I feel like I have nothing to contribute. My boyfriend wants to do things with me, like play tennis or go to the movies. I don't know why he still hangs around. I'm sure there are tons of more attractive and smarter women out there. I don't get him, you know.

C: You mentioned sleep, but what about your eating habits? Has anything changed? *[Chooses to ignore the additional self-criticism to stay on the topic of presenting symptoms].*

L: No, not really. I don't cook much but my boyfriend does. He likes to do it, so I eat what he makes, or I order out.

C: You said that you go to the gym regularly. Is that still the case? Have you tried anything else to cope with the fatigue and the other issues you talked about?

L: I still go to the gym. I like to go. I like to burn myself out. It's the only time I feel like I'm actually doing something real. Big accomplishment of my day (Lydia gives a little self-deprecating smirk). If I did anything else? I got a kitten. I like to watch him. It's about the only thing that makes me smile. Sometimes, I would just like to sit on my couch and watch him for a while. The big lazy potato watching her kitten play.

C: Do you have friends or family that you talk to sometimes? Have you talked about it with your boyfriend?

L: Not really. They all have their own stuff. I don't want to bother them. I try to act as if everything is fine. I don't want to burden others with my crap.

[Decides to use this time to move to Personal history and obtain more background information, as well as information regarding past psychological issues]

C: Lydia, you mentioned earlier that this wasn't the first time that you have felt this way. Can you tell me more about that?

L: Yeah I guess. I made two suicide attempts when I was in my early 20s. I had a bad breakup. I was really destroyed. I just couldn't seem to do anything. School was really overwhelming, especially when I started my Masters. So anyway, yeah, I felt really bad and I took some pills, but then I called 9-1-1 both times and they pumped my stomach.

C: Did you take any medications or go in therapy to help with these issues?

L: After the second time, yeah I took antidepressants. I still take them now. I also went in therapy with this guy. I don't know if he was a psychologist or a psychotherapist or a counselor. He just asked how I was doing. I don't really know what that accomplished. After a while, I just stopped going because I couldn't figure out what we were doing. Seemed like a big waste of time.

C: Yet you contacted me now that you are faced with a similar situation? *[Highlights potential contradiction and probes for potential ambivalence to treatment].*

L: Touché. Yeah I guess so. My doctor said it would be a good idea and he recommended you. I thought well, just because I saw a quack before doesn't mean they are all quacks. You have a Ph.D., so you have to know something, right?

C: Well, I hope so (smiling genuinely at Lydia). We'll find out, right? When you went through all that before, who was there that you could turn to?

L: My parents and my sister. A good friend from high school too. But I didn't want to bother them with this stuff.

C: How did they react when they found out about your suicide attempts?

L: They didn't. Nobody knows.

C: Are you feeling suicidal now? *[Screening for current suicidal risk].*

L: No, I'm done with that. It's not worth killing yourself over such trivial crap.

C: Given that you were able to keep this a secret from the people closest to you, how likely is it that you would tell me about it if you did feel suicidal?

L: Ha, ha, right. Well it's not the same. It's your job to hear about that stuff. I don't think I would have any problems telling you about it. I don't know what you could do about it, but I would probably still tell you.

C: Since you have had these depressive episodes in the past, have there been periods when you felt good?

L: Yeah, yeah for sure. I think that the first time it happened I was really young. I had just started university, I was in love. School was really overwhelming, and my boyfriend was so smart. I just always felt like I didn't measure up. When he left to go for a year abroad, we broke up. I wanted to wait for him, but he told me not to bother. That's when I started to feel depressed, I think. After my first suicide attempt, I finished my Bachelor degree and I guess I felt good about that; so I started a Masters. But, then, it was like everyone was so much smarter than me and I really felt like I made a huge mistake. That's when I went in this black hole. I didn't leave my room for so long. I think my parents were worried that time. Anyway, after the second suicide attempt and the therapy, or whatever that guy did, I decided I needed to pull up my socks. I mean: what do I have to feel bad about? I live in a free country, I can work, I am financially independent. I have no reason to feel bad about life. The only thing is that there's nothing special about me. That's it.

C: You have said that a couple of times already. Can you tell me what you mean about that?

L: Well, it's obvious, right? I am pretty average. Average height. Average size. Average intelligence. Average life. Nothing to see here.

C: In comparison to whom or what?

L: I don't know, people with more personality I guess. People with cool interests or abilities. I can't even whistle, or juggle, or anything else that I would define as very basic talents.

C: Have you always felt like that?

L: That's a good question. I don't know. I think it probably started when I was a teenager. You start to be much more self-conscious then. You spend more time thinking about yourself. I guess that's when it started. That and with the stuff with my sister.

C: Can you tell me more about her?

L: Yeah, sure. I have an older sister, two years older. We used to be really close. We shared a bedroom. She was my hero. She was always really intense, passionate, creative. When we were young, she started to have problems at school and then also at home. She would just lose her mind, scream at everyone, break stuff. She left notes under my pillow telling me that I was horrible and worthless. It was pretty bad. She used to be great at school, but then that all changed. My parents spent a lot of time and effort trying to help her. We all did. It looked like she was really suffering, you know. I tried to be good, not cause trouble. My parents had enough with her; so I just kinda disappeared in the background, tried to not attract too much attention. I don't like conflict.

C: How are things now? *[Bridging between exploring personal history and obtaining more information about ecosystemic factors].*

L: They're fine. My sister is doing her graduate work in Europe. I don't know if she'll drop out though. She's done that a couple of times already. She can't seem to find something that she can stick with. Life isn't as easy for her as it is for me, as she likes to remind me.

C: What about your parents?

L: They're fine too. They retired. My dad is pretty oblivious to everything. He pretty much checked out. He mostly plays golf all the time. My mom is a really anxious person. She calls me three times a day, and she gets hysterical if I don't pick up. She needs a hobby.

C: Are you close to them now?

L: Well, I go visit them every second weekend. They live about 2 hours away, so I take the bus. My parents don't like it if I don't visit often. They always have a full schedule planned: restaurants to try, a play to see, an exhibit to go to. It's all very structured. I skype with my sister about once a week. Just small talk mostly, but we are planning a trip together for early next year.

C: Lydia, what do you think are the biggest stressors in your life right now? *[Focusing on ecosystemic factors].*

L: That is the crux of it, right? Nothing really, except for work probably. I worry about how well I am doing at work. Otherwise, there is nothing really stressful in my life. I can pay my bills. I live alone with my cat. I have a low-key boyfriend and my family. That's it. There is no reason for me to feel bad, except that I feel bad all the time.

C: How do you make sense of that?

L: I don't, I really don't. That's why I'm here.

C: Can you tell me what matters most to you? What do you feel are your core values in life?

L: I think I have pretty high standards. I think it's important to hold yourself to high standards. That's why I feel so bad all the time, because I don't meet any of them. I think it's important to work hard, to be responsible for fixing your own problems, and not act like a victim. I think that people need to challenge themselves more. Society is turning into a bunch of morons. You just need to watch the television to see just how far we have gone.

C: So it sounds like you have a pretty clear image of the kind of things that you believe are important in life. Where does your boyfriend and your family fit in all this? *[Exploring potential sources of social and emotional support, as well as client's likelihood of accessing them].*

L: Well, family is important. I think that's a given. My boyfriend. . . . I don't know. We were friends before we started going out. He was the exact opposite of my ex. He is so laid-back, very calm, and very kind. He's warm, and he never asks for anything. I'm not sure what he sees in me sometimes, but he's just comfortable to be with.

C: Do you love him?

L: Yeah, I guess. Sometimes I'm not really sure what that means . . . I like being with him. I would be sad if he wasn't in my life. I guess that's love.

C: Are there other significant people in your life right now? Friends?

L: Not really. When I moved here a few years ago, I started to lose touch with my friends back home. I have what I would call acquaintances here, but like I said I don't really enjoy going out with them right now.

C: Yes, you mentioned that you felt like "you had nothing to contribute?"

L: Yeah, it just makes me really anxious when I'm in a group. I feel like if I say nothing, then I will look dumb and if I say something, then they will confirm that I am in fact dumb. It's a catch 22.

C: That sounds like that would be very stressful. Do you always feel anxious when you are in a social situation? *[Going back to confirm and expand on potential anxious symptomatology].*

L: Yes, I used to hate school presentations. I hate meetings at work too. I don't like having the spotlight on me.

C: Are there other things that make you feel anxious?

L: When my boss wants to talk to me. I'm always worried that I did a poor job. Sometimes my heart starts to race, and it's like I can't even really listen to what he is saying. I just feel cold sweat down my back and my hands get clammy.

C: That sounds like panic. Do you have trouble breathing or feel lightheaded?

L: No it doesn't get that bad. I had those when I was in university, but I haven't had a full-blown panic attack in years. It's just panic symptoms, and I usually just talk myself down.

C: What do you say to yourself?

L: Calm down. You can't lose your mind here. Just breathe and everything will be okay.

C: And it usually works?

L: Works well enough. Sometimes I go to the bathroom until I feel calmer or I'll go for a walk. There's a nice path behind our building and I can walk to the river from there.

C: You said earlier that your mom is a really anxious person and that she worries a lot. Do you find that you worry a lot about things too? *[Completing the symptoms inquiry to explore anxious symptomatology].*

L: Not really, I worry that I'm a failure, but that's it. I don't worry about things. Like I said, I don't have much to worry about. I don't have debt. My family is in good health. I'm not fat and I don't have health issues. There is no reason to worry about stuff, except for me. So it's all my fault.

C: You think of yourself as a failure?

L: Yup.

C: I find that interesting because sitting across from you, my first impressions are that you are a well-educated professional and financially independent young woman with considerable personal resources, good insight, and excellent verbal skills. I have only known you for about 30 minutes, but failure is not the term I would use to describe you. *[Probing for client's reaction to a soft confrontation to gently challenge her view of self].*

L: Uh, wait a while (smirks again and turns her head to the side to avoid eye contact).

C: I think I have made you uncomfortable. That wasn't my intent, Lydia.

L: No, no, it's fine. You're just being nice. Really it's okay. You're supposed to say stuff like that to help me with my mood, right?

C: Well, I do want to help you with your mood, and I also want to be as honest and as transparent as possible with you. I hope you'll feel the same with me as we learn about each other and our work together. I guess, maybe, sometimes the way we see ourselves can be very different than the way others perceive us. Maybe this is what is happening right now. *[Probing for insight, perspective taking, and exploring potential prognostic concerns related to interpersonal dynamics and rigidity of her intrapsychic difficulties].*

L: I get that. It's like when I say to my boyfriend that I don't get why he stays with me and he says that he wishes I could see myself the way he sees me. It's a bit corny, but I get it. Guess I fooled you too Doc, just saying (Lydia smiles shyly).

C: Okay, let's leave it at that for now then. You mentioned that you visited your family doctor recently. Are you seeing any other health professionals right now? *[Confirming who is part of the circle of care].*

L: No, that's it. Do you think I need to see anyone apart from you?

C: Not at the moment, but as we make a plan together to help you improve your coping and feel better, we may consider it. Is that alright?

L: Yeah, yeah for sure.

C: So we talked about a number of important issues in your life regarding your mood, anxiety, your work, and your relationships. I wonder how has it been so far talking with me today? *[Probing for insight and the capacity to form a working alliance].*

L: It's been good actually, easier than I thought it would be. You are good at making people comfortable. Guess that's a given in your line of work, but still . . . I appreciate it.

C: I am glad to hear it. I have really appreciated how forthcoming and insightful you are about what you have been coping with. (Lydia turns her head aside again to avoid eye contact) How does that land in your lap, Lydia?

L: Yeah, it lands pretty awkwardly actually. I don't really like compliments. They make me feel weird, like I want to jump out of my skin.

C: Mmmh, I see. Sometimes it's hard to hear things about ourselves, even good things coming from other people.

L: I don't like it from anyone, really. It's not about you.

C: Is this something you would like to work on?

L: What? Taking compliments?

C: Yes, exactly.

L: Ha ha, I never thought about it. Maybe, yes, maybe?

C: Maybe down the road?

L: Yes, down the road. Let's not start with that.

C: That's fair. So what would you like to start with? What is the most important thing for you right now? *[Assessing client motivation and potential goals for treatment]*.

L: Right now I need to get better so I can keep my job and not screw it up. That's what matters most.

C: Okay, that's fair and a really good place to start. Is there anything else you would like to work on? For instance, if therapy were successful, how do [you] see things changing for you down the road?

L: I'd like to not be such a potato, never doing anything. I'd like to have things to do and feel good about it. I'd like to feel like smiling more. I'd like to enjoy being around others more. I'd like to feel more confident.

C: That's a lot of goals! I like it! (Lydia gives a shy smile)

L: Yeah, maybe it's too much?

C: No, I think it's a good list. I think it shows good insight on your part, and I like that you know what you want. Lydia, here is what I understand from what you have told me so far *[Presents a short case formulation to the client]*: You have been coping for some time with both depressive and anxious symptoms. I think it's a testament to your own resilience that you haven't needed more support until now. It sounds to me like the reason for both these depressive and anxious symptoms have been around for some time, perhaps since adolescence or even childhood. It sounds like it was a pretty stressful experience at home growing up, especially given your sister's own struggles and your focus on trying to not cause any additional stress to your family. It seems that you probably learned from a young age that it was important to be good, work hard, and deal with things on your own, because your parents had enough to manage already. It certainly sounds like they had their plate full, but I wonder if it might also have sent the unintended message that you had to deal with your stuff on your own and it was your responsibility to do so? Now, there is nothing wrong with relying on yourself, but we all need help once in a while. This is why I also want to really make it clear that I think you showed excellent judgment by seeking help from your family doctor now, and that you were so proactive in asking to meet with me. Does that make sense so far?

L: I guess so. I haven't really thought much before about how my problems could come from when I was growing up. Sometimes it feels like psychologists always bring things back to your childhood, but I think it could make sense. I'm willing to consider it.

C: Okay, so let's say that this is a hypothesis right now. Maybe it's the case, maybe it's not. But we'll consider it and see if it turns out that it rings true. The other part is that I am hearing a good deal of self-criticism in what you shared with me. I think that you can be pretty hard on yourself. I know you said that it was important for you to have high standards, and I certainly have no problem with that, but I wonder if there is a way to have high standards and to be kinder to yourself. How does that sound?

L: Yeah, maybe. I'm not exactly sure what you mean by that.

C: Fair enough. Here's what I think: what we think and how we think has a big influence on our actions and on our mood. If you tell yourself 20 times per day that you are a loser, chances are you won't feel like a winner. Right?

L: Yeah, I get that.

C: The problem is that this kind of language is not very helpful. First, it might be wrong, as in perhaps you are not a loser. Again, this is a hypothesis that I would like us to consider. Second, saying that you are a loser does nothing to turn you into a winner. Right?

L: Yes, that is a good point.

C: So I think that addressing your self-talk, the way you think about yourself, and talk about yourself might be very important to helping you alleviate your depressive and anxious symptoms. Basically, maybe you shouldn't believe everything you think!

L: So I am the problem? I was right!

C: Well, your self-talk might be part of the problem. The great thing is you are also at the heart of the solution. And as we might uncover, this part of you that criticizes you seems to have good values or standards (for example, work and personal ethics), but it seems to be on overdrive and not allowing you to see how resourceful and meaningful you are. It's like this part takes too much space and prevents you from being to see and receive what is good about you.

L: Right, so my problems may have been there for a long time, and the way I think about myself is making things worse.

C: Yes, these are hypotheses I'd like us to explore. And I think these two parts connect to what has happened since your promotion. I think that when good things happen to you, it is very scary. Does that resonate with you?

L: Yes, a lot. I don't like surprises, even good ones. I am always waiting for the other shoe to drop.

C: Right, so I think that you have this view of yourself that is quite negative, and I think that you are fearful that you won't measure up and that others will judge you in the same manner that you judge yourself. So this causes anxiety and over time, contributes to a more depressed mood. What do you think of that?

L: I think it makes sense. What do I do about it?

C: Okay, here is what I would suggest we do (takes a piece of paper and a pen). If it's alright with you, I'd like to write this out for us. *[Begins to present the three spheres of the treatment plan].*

L: Sure, go ahead.

C: I believe that we need to focus on three areas or spheres. The first one (draws a circle on the paper) relates to self-care and your capacity to cope with stress. You already mentioned that you go to the gym, which is excellent because we know that exercise can help with mood. I also took note of the fact that you adopted a kitten recently. Pets can also be a good mood booster and they can help us relax and self-soothe by letting us pet them and cuddle with them. It's a really good thing.

L: Yeah, he is a little fur ball that just wants to cuddle all the time. He is ridiculous, but I like putting him in my lap and scratching him behind the ears.

C: That's good. I think you should do that as much as you can, in fact. Now, there are other things we can do to help with your mood and your self-care. I would like us to work on a list of pleasant activities that you can pick from to do on a daily basis. It could also be really beneficial for you to go out at least once a day and take a walk. You said you were off work, and I think it's really important that you don't spend that time simply at home on your couch.

L: Like a big potato. . . .

C: Well, sometimes taking it easy and relaxing in front of the T.V. is good, but too much of it isn't. It's important to make sure you go out and smell the roses. Is there anywhere near where you live that would be pleasant to walk?

L: Yes, there's a couple of footpaths behind my building that connect to where people go jogging in the park. I could easily take a walk there. It's actually pretty nice, but I haven't been in some time.

C: Great, can you see yourself doing it at least once a day?

L: Yes, I don't see why not—maybe if it rains, then I don't know that I'd like to do that.

C: Okay, well as long as it's not raining hard then?

L: Yeah, okay.

C: I also think it's important that you keep a regular sleep schedule, even though you are off work. It might be tempting to sleep at all hours of the day because you have nowhere to be, but sticking to a regular sleep schedule is a better way of ensuring that you are rested, reenergized, and in a better mood. What do you think about that?

L: Yeah, it's tempting to take naps during the day, but I can try to stick to a regular sleep schedule.

C: What about eating habits? Is there anything that we should be concerned about?

L: No, I eat my fruits and vegetables daily. I don't like fast food, and I don't drink alcohol. It makes me sick.

C: What about smoking?

L: No, I don't smoke. I smoked marijuana when I was a teenager, but not since then.

C: Okay, what about drugs? Street drugs? Prescription drugs?

L: No, none of that. I take vitamins: a daily multivitamin and a vitamin D, because I heard it could help with mood.

C: And apart from the antidepressants you are taking, is there anything else?

L: No, well, my doctor offered to give me a prescription for Valium, but I declined. I need to deal with anxiety, not numb myself.

C: Fair enough. Are you taking your antidepressant as prescribed by your doctor?

L: Yes, I take them at night before bed every day. It's part of my routine now. I don't forget.

C: You also mentioned that your boyfriend has been trying to get you to do "fun" things with him. What kind of things do you usually enjoy doing with him?

L: I like to play tennis, but we haven't once this year. There's a court right outside our building.

C: Do you both have tennis equipment?

L: Yup. Just gathering dust in the front closet for the moment.

C: Okay, I'd like you to try and go play tennis with him once a week. Can you do it?

L: If it's my homework, I'll do it.

C: Great, then consider it your homework. So we have talked about pleasant activities, going to the gym, going for walks, keeping a regular sleep schedule and good eating habits, and playing tennis with your boyfriend. I wrote all this down in the "self-care" sphere. We'll revisit this later to add and change as necessary to make sure we have a good regimen in place to help you improve your mood and develop your capacity for self-care.

L: Okay.

C: Lydia, I am starting with focusing on this sphere, because building up your coping and self-care is at the base of this process. When you are stressed, anxious, and depressed, it's like you take water out of your well or you are depleting your battery. If you don't proactively fill that well back up or you don't take time to recharge your battery, it runs dry. Once you have reached that point, it's a lot harder to get back up and it creates more instability in your mood. What I want to do with you is to develop consistent strategies for you to implement in your routine so the well does not run dry all the time. How does that sound?

L: It makes sense. I get what you're saying. If I don't do anything good for myself, then I'll never feel good.

C: That's right. There are two other areas that I'd like us to work on together, but I don't want to overwhelm you with information right now. I'll just go over these more generally, and once we feel like we have a better handle on the self-care sphere, we can start to implement strategies in these two other spheres. Is that alright?

L: Yes, I agree that you have already given me a lot of homework, and I don't know how much more I could do right now.

C: Exactly. The point is to help you feel better, not run you ragged!

L: Right, right, glad to hear it.

C: Okay, so the second sphere of interest relates to your sense of yourself as being in control or not in your life. You know how some people really feel like they are in charge and others feel more like they are at the mercy of fate?

L: Yeah, absolutely. I am probably more the latter.

C: Right, so that is something else I think we could work on together, that is to help you feel more like you're the one sitting in the driver's seat. This could involve looking at the way you think about things, helping you develop alternative ways to look at and address things that come up, so that over time, you can feel more control over the important parts of your life.

L: That sounds good, but I'm not sure how to do it.

C: That's fine. This is something we can do together.

L: Okay, we can talk about this once I have done my homework?

C: Yes, exactly. Now the last sphere I would like to talk about is the one that relates to your relationships and the way you interact with others. The first sphere was about helping you develop a more sustainable life hygiene. The second sphere was about helping you develop your sense of self-efficacy and control over your life. The last sphere relates to the way we connect with others (draws bidirectional arrows between all three spheres). Do you see how the three spheres relate to one another?

L: Yeah I guess it's all connected, right?

C: Yes, that's correct. The last sphere is about helping you feel more confident when you interact with others and to help you develop and maintain more satisfying relationships. Does that sound like something you would like to do?

L: Yes, of course. I do feel pretty alone most of the time. I don't really talk to anyone about things. I am so concerned by the way they will perceive me that I prefer to keep things to myself.

C: I understand that opening yourself may feel pretty risky.

L: It does. It really does.

C: Okay, so I would not force you to do anything you don't want to do. I am a firm believer that usually people are afraid of things for a good reason. We may not have all the information today to understand why it feels so risky right now, but I think this is something worth exploring. If we understand where it comes from, we might be able to do something about it. How does that sound?

L: It sounds good, it sounds really good actually. I don't know that I believe that you can do it, but I guess it's worth a try.

C: Excellent. I can understand that this might seem like a pretty tall order right now, but you know what they say: "every journey begins with a single step." We will take things one at a time and go from there. *[Checking in to see how the client responds to the proposed treatment plan and motivation for change].*

L: Alright, sure.

C: At the same time, it is really important to take these initial steps, because nothing changes as long as nothing changes. You know what I mean?

L: Yeah, actions speak louder than words. If I don't do my homework, it's not gonna work.

C: Well, let's say that it will be a lot harder to change things, but I want us to follow your lead. I won't push you to do things you aren't ready for, and the changes we will discuss are those that you can get on board with. After all, it's your life Lydia, you should be making the choices as to how you want things to change or stay the same. *[Focusing on developing working alliance and collaborative agreement for treatment plan].*

L: Yeah, but I think I could use the input. I don't know that I've made great decisions so far.

C: Well, that is certainly something we can talk about. How do you feel about our first session? *[Checking in for client feedback about the session and socializing client regarding obtaining regular feedback about treatment plan].*

L: Like I said before, pretty good overall. A little intimidated by the work ahead, but I like how structured and clear things are. Can I keep that piece of paper?

C: Absolutely. I also want you to know that I'll be tracking your mood and anxiety over our sessions and that I will likely check in with you on a regular basis to make sure that the plan we have in place still makes sense. It's important that we adjust things as needed so we can ensure that the strategies we focus on are the most appropriate right now. I am always open to your feedback, good or bad. If you feel like treatment is not helping you or you don't feel comfortable with me, please do not hesitate to let me know about it. The more you let me in on these things, the quicker I can adjust how I work with you. I am a good psychologist, but I am certainly not perfect *[Explaining the importance of treatment monitoring and how it will be accomplished; explaining the importance of feedback about treatment and the alliance and modeling a more balanced view of self].*

L: Okay, that makes sense.

C: Great, so let's look at when you can come in for your next session.

CHAPTER 8

The Supervision and Evaluation of Assessment and Treatment Planning Competency Development

In the previous chapters, we offered the conceptual and theoretical underpinnings for the promotion of integrative approaches to assessment and treatment planning. We also advocated for the need to ground clinical practice within an evidence-based, patient-centered approach that includes an interprofessional focus. Finally, we spoke at length of the importance of professional ethics, professionalism, and self-reflective practice as corner stones for professional development and competency building.

Then, we presented our model for structuring both psychological assessment and treatment planning meetings, illustrating core principles and techniques with two extensive case vignettes. Now, we turn our attention to a central process underlying the development of competency in psychological assessment and treatment planning—clinical supervision and evaluation. The apprenticeship model of supervision in the helping professions has been relied upon heavily since ancient Greek times (Milne, 2009). In fact, the great majority of graduate students in clinical psychology programs in North America spend about a third of their training in supervision (Greenman, Gosselin, Barker and Grenier, 2015).

First, let us define what supervision is: "It is an activity/intervention provided by a more senior member to more junior members of that same organization. It can be a planned or unplanned activity that can occur one-on-one or in a group format. This relationship is evaluative, extends over time, and has the simultaneous purpose of enhancing professional functioning and supporting the well-being of the more junior members, while monitoring the quality of services/research" (adapted from Falender et al., 2004). Supervision also includes a number of important roles as follows:

- Administrative/evaluative role: managing day-to-day activities, completing performance appraisals.
- Monitoring/consulting role: overseeing case management, consulting on how to address specific issues as needed.
- Didactic/training role: teaching knowledge, modeling behaviors, and techniques.
- Mentoring/professional development role: offering guidance, feedback, and career development advice.
- Counseling/supportive role: fostering a safe working environment, offering appropriate emotional support in challenging times.

Supervisors are usually the first to observe the clinical work of graduate students and early career clinicians, and they spend a considerable amount of time shaping and providing feedback on the focus, manner, and content of their trainee's clinical interventions. They are most often the ones responsible for grounding their trainees' clinical work within evidence-based practice, to foster competency building up to and past minimal licensing requirements, to model interprofessional deportment, and to participate in their overall professional development. As such, supervisors are instrumental in the competent application of the model we have outlined here.

In their seminal article on principles for training in evidence-based psychology (Beck et al., 2014), Beck advocates for four core principles, which include: (1) teaching students to base clinical practice on research, (2) teaching critical thinking, (3) teaching lifelong learning, and (4) integrating experiential with didactic learning in all aspects of training. To accomplish these objectives, the authors recommend that supervisors provide guidance relating to searching the research literature relevant to cases seen by supervisees, critically appraise findings in terms of validity and patient-centered care, and use this appraisal to guide both the assessment and treatment planning process. As such, supervisors are identified as key agents of training in evidence-based practice. This type of approach is illustrated in a recent study (Callahan, 2015), which presented the results of a teaching intervention made to improve the technical skills training in pre-practicum psychological assessment competencies. The authors created a conceptual map that integrated ongoing feedback with sequential, cumulative, and increasingly complex practice of assessment measures within a professional doctoral program in clinical psychology. The authors found that this approach resulted in fewer errors over time, as well as higher competency ratings from supervisors at the end of the assessment training period. This study illustrates well the relationship between evidence-based training and clinical competency development, as well as the central role of the supervisor in helping trainees bridge the gap between knowledge and practice.

Over the last decade, assessment skills have been consistently identified as a core clinical competency within professional psychology. In one of its most recent iteration, this set of clinical competencies has been defined within the professional psychology competency framework as including the following:

1. The application of knowledge of individual and cultural characteristics in assessment and diagnosis;
2. The application of evidence-based criteria in selection and use of assessment methods (including understanding of psychometric properties, cost-effectiveness issues, and relevance to a particular person);
3. The demonstration of familiarity with models and techniques of interviewing;
4. The selection or development of assessment instruments based on available normed data and criterion-reference standards (including limits of these instruments for particular assessment situations);
5. The administration and scoring of assessment instruments that follows best practices guidelines and current psychometric research;

6. The interpretation and synthesis of results from multiple sources that follow best practices guidelines and current psychometric research;

7. The formulation of a diagnostic recommendation or professional opinion using relevant best practices in assessment and considering all assessment information provided by the person who is being assessed as well as collateral sources (including professionals from other disciplines);

8. The communication of assessment results in an integrative manner;

9. The evaluation of effectiveness of psychological services to communities and organizations; and

10. The reception of assessment training that includes the development and communication of formative and summative supervisee evaluation (Rodolfa et al., 2013).

Setting and monitoring training goals for assessment competency development

In her recent book on successful supervision, Lee (2012) proposes a framework that includes five elements that interact to predict success in supervision, based on her extensive interviews with academic supervisors. First, she states that supervision must be functional, that is that the supervisor is a provider of rules and regulations and he/she must provide necessary guidance and information for the trainee to do their work. Second, she proposes that supervision also encompasses an enculturation role, wherein the supervisor acts as a gatekeeper and role model for the profession, as well as a liaison to his/her network of connections. Third, Lee asserts that successful supervision encourages critical thinking by challenging the trainee's work, encouraging stronger arguments, and a more clearly expressed analysis of their work. Fourth, she also discusses the process of emancipation that can occur within successful supervision where the supervisor acts as a mentor, supporting personal growth and encouraging self-reflective practice in trainees. Finally, successful supervision is anchored in a relationship development process where supervision is conceptualized as a team effort that can become more collegial over time, as trainees become professionals.

This framework provides a useful structure to ground supervision practices in, but it lacks a clear presentation of the manner in which supervisors may achieve these outcomes with trainees. To help us is this endeavor, we turn to Wade and Jones' more recent book on strength-based clinical supervision (2015). The authors suggest that successful supervision begins with setting goals. Indeed, they introduce this idea with the following image: "imagine trying to learn archery without being able to see if you have ever hit the target? To say the least, it would be very difficult" (p. 95).

In their strength-based framework, they stress the idea that setting goals and providing feedback and evaluation are inherently connected. First, goals direct attention and effort toward goal-relevant activities and away from goal-irrelevant activities. Second, goals can be energizing, and higher goals can lead to greater effort than lower goals (although the highest level of effort occurs when the task is moderately difficult, that is in the zone of *proximal development*). Third, goals affect persistence, and challenging goals tend to prolong effort. Goal specificity is highly important to effective goal-setting because it reduces ambiguity, and the trainee can more easily apply the knowledge and skills they already have when they know specifically what is expected of them. In addition, simply urging trainees to do their best is usually less effective than setting specific goals. Finally, goals can affect action indirectly by leading to arousal, discovery, and the generation of self-efficacy with the attainment of moderately difficult goals, which in turn is correlated with enhanced goal commitment (Wade and Jones, 2015).

Based on this premise, the authors also present a clear set of steps designed to collaboratively create supervisee goals within the supervision process. Once a safe and welcoming environment has been established between supervisor and trainee, supervisors are encouraged to assess supervisee learning goals. The objective is to use positive, open-ended questions to elicit preferences, passions, and strengths. Supervisors can then establish baselines and identify relevant competencies to focus on by assessing the current clinical experience of their supervisees and collaborating with them to create a vision of what the supervisee might become through the learning process. Based on this discussion, practical steps can be formulated to implement identified aspirations and goals within reason, given the particular opportunities and contingencies offered by the training setting. Working within the zone of proximal development, the supervisor is then encouraged to provide frequent and specific positive and critical feedback on the areas and competencies identified as training goals. In this context, the supervisor is encouraged to challenge the supervisee to proactively raise their internal bar of self-expectations, to maximize professional development. A number of effective supervision techniques can be used to reach these outcomes, including: listening, observing, managing, supporting, questioning, formulating, feeding back, challenging, disagreeing, evaluating, guiding experiential learning (through modeling and role-play), and reviewing documentation.

These steps are highly consistent with what Guerin et al. (2015) have identified as the three main characteristics of "excellent supervisors." First, they employ a broad range of approaches informed by their experience of being supervised. Second, they place great importance on their relationship with students. Third, they reveal a strong awareness of their own responsibilities in actively developing the emerging professional identities of their trainees.

In accordance with these recommendations, we also propose a number of suggestions to supervisees, based on Falender and Shafranske's (2012) book on participating in clinical supervision. Before beginning supervision, it is important for trainees to reflect on their own expectations of their supervisor. How do they approach working with a new supervisor? How do they convey their openness to experience and feedback? Supervision is a time-consuming and intensive process that requires preparation. It is necessary to review relevant materials, complete assigned tasks, and ask for help when needed so that supervisees can arrive prepared to participate fully in supervision meetings. During these meetings, supervisees are strongly encouraged to listen carefully and to ask for clarification when they do not understand. They should also follow through on suggestions made by their supervisors, even when that may seem challenging at times. Supervision should be a training priority, and supervisees should treat it as such.

To help their supervisor orient them effectively, supervisees should reflect to identify the strategies that work best for their own learning, based on their past training and learning experience. Supervisees also need to take responsibility for their own professional development by seeking out resources and readings, within and outside supervision. Finally, before trying out new things in practice, it is highly recommended that ideas are first introduced in supervision to receive feedback from their supervisor.

Evaluating Assessment Competency Development

Closely tied to goal setting and feedback is the evaluation of clinical competencies. Supervision feedback provided on a regular basis, focused on mutually agreed-upon specific goals, is key to competency-based professional development. Competency-based evaluation can play a central role in achieving this goal by providing a map to supervisors and supervisees about observable knowledge, skills, and attitudes that are typical of assessment and treatment planning competencies, as well as other related clinical competencies, such as professionalism, ethics, self-reflective practice, and interprofessional competence at each developmental stage. We provide here an example of a competency-based evaluation form used in a professional doctoral program (see Appendix A).

Such a form can help orient initial supervisor–supervisee discussion around goal setting and provide specific targets for professional development and feedback. In addition, because supervisors are simply expected to check off what they observe, they can provide a much more nuanced evaluation of the knowledge, skills, and attitudes they have observed their supervisees demonstrate over time, which can include behaviors that span multiple developmental levels, thereby creating a goal-setting and evaluation process that is more realistic and reflective of the complex training experience that is typical in professional psychology graduate training programs.

References

Beck, J.G., Castonguay, L.G., Chronis-Tuscano, A., Klonsky, E.D., McGinn, L.K., and Youngstrom, E.A. (2014). Principles for training in evidence-based psychology: Recommendations for the graduate curricula in Clinical Psychology, Clinical Psychology: Science and Practice, 21 (4), 410-424.

Callahan, J.L. (2015). Evidence-based technical skills training in pre-practicum psychological assessment, Training and Education in Professional Psychology, 9 (1), 21-27.

Falender, C. A., Cornish, J. A., Goodyear, R., Hatcher, R., Kaslow, N. J., Leventhal, G., . . . Grus, C. (2004). Defining competencies in psychology supervision: A consensus statement. Journal of Clinical Psychology, 60, 771–785.

Falender, C.A. and Shafranske, E.P. (2012). Getting the most out of clinical training and supervision: a guide for practicum students and interns, APA Books.

Greenman, P., Gosselin, J., Barker, K. and Grenier, J. (2015). La psychologie clinique en soins primaires : implications pour le développement professionnel des psychologues [*Clinical Psychology in Primary Care : Implications for the professional development of psychologists*], In Gosselin, J., Greenman, P. and Joanisse, M. (Eds.). Le développement professionnel en soins de santé primaires au Canada: nouveaux défis [*Professional Development in Primacy Care in Canada : New Challenges*], Presses de l'Université du Québec, 129-144.

Guerin, C., Kerr, H, and Green, I. (2015). Supervision strategies: narratives from the field, Teaching in Higher Education, 20 (1), 107-118.

Lee, A. (2012). Successful research supervision: advising students doing research, Routledge/Taylor and Francis Group: London and New York.

Milne, D.L. (2009). Evidence-Based Clinical Supervision: Principles and Practice, Wiley/Blackwell.

Rodolfa, E., Greenberg, S., Hunsley, J., Smith-Zoetler, M., Cox, D., Sammons, M., Caro, C., and Spivak, H. (2013). A competency model for the practice of Psychology, Training and Education in Professional Psychology, 7 (2), 71-83.

Wade, J.C. and Jones, J.E. (2015). Strength-based clinical supervision : a positive psychology approach to clinical training, Springer Publishing Company: New York.

APPENDIX A

A Framework for Competency-Based Evaluation of the Integrative and Interprofessional Model of Assessment and Treatment Planning

This evaluation form serves two purposes: (1) Through the use of competency-based anchors, supervisors and trainees can come to a common understanding of trainee performance and specifically target the skills needed to achieve the desired competency level within an area of practice within a specified time frame (i.e., midpoint and final evaluation). (2) Through the written commentary, trainees are provided with an overall evaluation of their performance during the training period covered by the evaluation. This evaluation is adapted from the Memorial University of Newfoundland Psy.D. Practicum Student Evaluation form (permission granted by Dr. Julie Gosselin, Clinical Training Director, 2016), which is based on the competency benchmarks document (Fouad, 2009) and aspects of The Ottawa Hospital Internship Evaluation Form (permission granted by Dr. Kerri Ritchie, Clinical Training Director, 2015), and the University of Rochester Medical Center Psychology Student Competency Assessment (permission granted by Dr. Jennifer West, Training Director, 2012).

Foundational competencies are the knowledge, skills, attitudes, and values that serve as the foundation for the functions a psychologist is expected to carry out as follows:

1. Science
   a. Scientific Mindedness and Clinical Application of Research
2. Professionalism
   a. Self-Reflective Practice and Interpersonal Functioning
   b. Ethics and Professional Standards
   c. Individual and Cultural Diversity
3. Relationships
   a. Professional Deportment
   b. Consultation and Functioning in Interprofessional Systems

Functional competencies are the functions or actions that a psychologist is expected to carry out as follows:

1. Assessment and Treatment Planning
   a. Psychological Assessment and Diagnostic Skills
   b. Treatment Planning Skills
2. Supervision
   a. Participation in Supervision Process
   b. Professional Development: Efficiency and Prioritization

Competencies are evaluated through behavioral anchor statements, which fall within five categories. Students, however, may fall completely within one of these five categories or levels of competence, or they may evidence behaviors and actions that fall within more than one competency level:

Advanced Skills: Level of supervision: Minimal; Focus of supervision: Largely self-reflective practice; Typical timing of this rating: Post-doctoral training or Psychology Board registration year. Skills and performance consistently meet the expected practice standards of the profession with minimal supervisory guidance, and the student is able to fully engage in self-reflective practice. This rating might be expected at the completion of postdoctoral training or the Psychology Board registration year. However, it is possible that some interns and advanced practicum students will be functioning at this level within some of the competency areas.

High Intermediate Skills: Level of supervision: provision of overall management of activities but depth will vary; Focus of supervision: based upon clinical need; Typical timing of rating: End of internship or advanced practica. Competency attained in all but most complex cases; students demonstrate sophisticated and refined clinical skills and generally meet all expected professional standards of practice. Supervisors still provide overall management of students' activities; however, the depth of supervision is based on specific clinical needs (e.g., some areas will require very little oversight, whereas others may be the focus of more in-depth feedback). This rating might be expected at the end of the Internship or of some advanced practica.

Intermediate Skills/Performance: Level of supervision: routine; Focus of supervision: refining and expanding professional and clinical skills; Typical timing of rating: during advanced practica or beginning of internship. Able to identify and meet expected professional standards but may need prompting, may not apply consistently, or may not understand nuance or complexity of issues. Most common rating during practica and at the beginning of internship. Routine supervision of clinical activities has a focus on refining and expanding professional and clinical skills.

Novice Skills/Performance: Level of supervision: regular supervisory guidance required; Focus of supervision: identify and build the requisite skills to meet standards; Typical timing of rating: during junior practica or for specialized skills in advanced practica. Meets part of the expected professional standards of practice, and/or requires supervisory guidance to identify and build the requisite skills to meet standards. Most common rating for junior practicum. However, it would not be uncommon for a senior practicum student or an intern learning a new area to be performing as a novice (e.g., couples' therapy, group therapy).

Does not Meet Expectations: Level of supervision: intensive supervision or remediation required; Focus of supervision: to attain acceptable level of competency consistent with expected professional standards of practice; Typical timing of rating: could occur at any point in training. Intensive remediation required to attain acceptable level of competency consistent with expected professional standards of practice. Implementation of an action plan is necessary with measurable objectives to guide the acquisition of requisite skills.

Supervisors are invited to check the statement(s) that most closely reflect the trainee's behaviors *most of the time* during their experience on practicum/internship. Supervisors may check more than one statement (in different skill levels) if the behavior of the trainee is not consistent, or if they feel that they are exhibiting behaviors that are not all at the same skill level for the same competency domain. Some of the categories may not be applicable to all aspects of training, and these categories include a check box for N/A. Supervisors are asked to complete all other categories.

The following are all recommended evaluation methods: (1) direct observation, (2) case discussion, (3) self-assessment, (4) video review, (5) 360-degree feedback, (6) chart review, and (7) supervisee self-evaluations. Some of these methods lend themselves better to the assessment of particular competencies. For example, the demonstration of clinical skills can be best observed through video review, direct observation, and case discussion. On the other hand, 360-degree feedback would be more appropriate for the assessment of competencies in the area of consultation and functioning in interprofessional systems. Supervisors should use various modalities of evaluation methods at their disposal to assess the development of assessment-related competencies, of which direct observation is always strongly recommended as best practice.

Foundational Competencies: 1. Scientific Knowledge

A. Scientific Mindedness and Clinical Application of Research	Mid	End
Advanced Skills/Performance:		
• Independently assesses problems and applies scientific knowledge and skills appropriately and habitually to develop solutions.	☐	☐
• Actively seeks out scrutiny of others for own work.	☐	☐
High Intermediate Skills/Performance:		
• Articulates, in supervision and case conference, support for his/her perspective derived from the literature.	☐	☐
• Formulates appropriate questions regarding case conceptualization.	☐	☐
• Generates appropriate hypotheses regarding own contribution to therapeutic process and outcome.	☐	☐
• Performs scientific critique of literature.	☐	☐
Intermediate Skills/Performance:		
• Needs some supervisory guidance to synthesize the information and conclusions that have been obtained from the literature.	☐	☐
• Generates hypotheses but is unsure how or reluctant to express their clinical judgment about their contribution to therapeutic process and outcome.	☐	☐
Novice Skills/Performance:		
• Aware of need for evidence to support hypotheses, but needs assistance to bring forward.	☐	☐
• Needs supervisory support/direction to perform scientific critique of literature and to connect this information to clinical practice.	☐	☐
Does not Meet Expectations:		
• Has significant difficulty presenting own work for scrutiny of others i.e., taping sessions, receiving and incorporating feedback, and/or utilizing outcome measures.	☐	☐
• Minimizes the importance of research in clinical practice.	☐	☐

Foundational Competencies: 2. Professionalism

A. Self-Reflective Practice and Interpersonal Functioning	Mid	End
Advanced Skills/Performance:		
• Typically demonstrates congruence between own and others' assessment and seeks to resolve any incongruities.	☐	☐
• Models appropriate self-care, monitors and evaluates attitudes, values and beliefs toward diverse others.	☐	☐
• Consistently anticipates and self-identifies disruptions in functioning and intervenes at an early stage/with minimal support from supervisors.	☐	☐
High Intermediate Skills/Performance:		
• Recognizes impact of self on others:		
• Able to describe how others experience him/her and identifies roles he/she might play within team or with colleagues in the workplace.	☐	☐
• Systematically and effectively reviews own professional performance with supervisors.	☐	☐
• Effectively determines when response to patient needs takes precedence over personal needs.	☐	☐
• Works with supervisor to monitor and identify early markers of fatigue and stress and takes action for self-care to ensure effective practice.	☐	☐
Intermediate Skills/Performance:		
• Supervisor occasionally needs to address the effect of stressors on professional functioning.	☐	☐
• Supervisor occasionally needs to address increasing insight with respect to how others experience him/her and identifies roles one might play within team or with colleagues in the workplace.	☐	☐
• Responsively utilizes supervision to enhance reflectivity and self-care.	☐	☐
Novice Skills/Performance:		
• With supervisory support, demonstrates openness to consider own personal concerns and issues to enhance recognition of their impact on others.	☐	☐
• Needs assistance and support to understand importance of self-care for effective practice.	☐	☐
Does not Meet Expectations:		
• Intensive remediation is required, with considerable structure and incremental measurable objectives, to address the awareness of impact of self on others and reflecting upon self.	☐	☐
• Frequent supervision is required to address the effect of stressors on professional functioning.	☐	☐

Foundational Competencies: 2. Professionalism

B. Ethics and Professional Standards	Mid	End
Advanced Skills/Performance:		
• Independently and consistently identifies ethical and legal issues.	☐	☐
• Takes independent and proactive action to correct situations that are in conflict with professional values and/or ethical principles.	☐	☐
• Judgment is reliable about when consultation is needed.	☐	☐
High Intermediate Skills/Performance:		
• Identifies ethical dilemmas effectively, actively consults with supervisor to act upon ethical and legal aspects of practice.	☐	☐
• Demonstrates ability to share, discuss, and address failures and lapses in adherence to professional values and ethical principles with supervisors/faculty as appropriate.	☐	☐
Intermediate Skills/Performance:		
• Generally recognizes situations in which ethical and legal issues might be pertinent.	☐	☐
• Supervision focus centers on refining one or more of the following:		
• Application of specific regulations and ethical guidelines in a particular workplace	☐	☐
• Identification of when supervisor input is needed	☐	☐
Novice Skills/Performance Level:		
• Displays basic understanding of core values and general knowledge of ethical principles.	☐	☐
• With supervision, displays capacity for appropriate boundary management, implements ethical concepts into professional behavior.	☐	☐
• Needs supervisory input to apply ethical principles in specific situations.	☐	☐
Does not Meet Expectations:		
• Has difficulty managing appropriate boundaries	☐	☐
• Is often unaware of legal issues, professional standards, and ethical principles	☐	☐
• Minimizes personal responsibility	☐	☐

Foundational Competencies: 2. Professionalism

C. Individual and Cultural Diversity	Mid	End
Advanced Skills/Performance:		
• Regularly and independently uses knowledge of the role of diversity in interactions to monitor and improve effectiveness as a professional.	☐	☐
• Communications and actions convey sensitivity to individual experience and needs while retaining professional demeanor and deportment.	☐	☐
• Respectful of the beliefs and values of colleagues even when inconsistent with personal beliefs and values.	☐	☐
High Intermediate Skills/Performance:		
• Critically evaluates feedback and initiates supervision regularly about diversity issues and contextual factors and puts this knowledge into practice.	☐	☐
• Displays respect in interpersonal interactions with others including those from divergent perspectives or backgrounds.	☐	☐
Intermediate Skills/Performance:		
• Articulates appropriate attitudes, values, and beliefs toward diverse others.	☐	☐
• Supervision needed to expand awareness and effective practice in relation to diversity issues.	☐	☐
Novice Skills/Performance:		
• Demonstrates knowledge, awareness, and understanding of the ways diversity and context shape interactions between and within individuals.	☐	☐
• Incorporation of concepts related to diversity and sensitivity in clinical practice is supported through supervisory guidance.	☐	☐
Does not Meet Expectations:		
• Demonstrates very limited knowledge, awareness, and/ or openness to the understanding of the ways in which diversity and context shape interactions between and within individuals.	☐	☐
• Intensive remediation is required to properly address diversity in clinical practice and/or professional relations.	☐	☐

Foundational Competencies: 3. Relationships

A. Professional Deportment	Mid	End
Advanced Skills/Performance:		
• Verbal and nonverbal communications are appropriate to the professional context including in challenging interactions.	☐	☐
• Independently accepts personal responsibility across settings and contexts.	☐	☐
• Effectively negotiates conflictual, difficult, and complex relationships including those with individuals and groups who differ significantly from oneself.	☐	☐
• Accepts and implements feedback from others.	☐	☐
• Shares feedback regularly and effectively with peers and supervisors relating to their own clinical work as well as the work of other team members.	☐	☐
High Intermediate Skills/Performance:		
• Forms effective working alliance with patients, supervisors, team members, and colleagues.	☐	☐
• Makes appropriate disclosures regarding problematic interpersonal situations	☐	☐
• Acknowledges own role in difficult interactions, including acknowledgment of own errors.	☐	☐
• Demonstrates emerging ability to share constructive feedback with peers and supervisors.	☐	☐
• Completes required case documentation promptly and accurately; accepts responsibility for meeting deadlines.	☐	☐
Intermediate Skills/Performance:		
• Utilizes appropriate language and demeanor in professional communications.	☐	☐
• Appropriately seeks input from supervisors when interpersonal concerns arise.	☐	☐
• Completes required case documentation needing some support in creating timelines and prioritizing competing task demands	☐	☐
Novice Skills/Performance:		
• Supervision focuses on transferring general interpersonal skills to the work environment and a broad array of people.	☐	☐
• Listens and is empathic with others, respects and shows interest in others' experiences, values, points of view, goals, etc.	☐	☐
• Needs guidance regarding the impact behavior has on patient and profession in general.	☐	☐
• Listens to and acknowledges feedback from others	☐	☐
• Needs prompting to complete case documentation and/or is required to submit numerous drafts due to errors.	☐	☐

(Continued)

Does not Meet Expectations:		
• Difficulty interacting effectively with individuals, groups, and/or communities.	☐	☐
• Does not seem to be aware of the impact of behavior on patient, profession or public (limited self-awareness of behavior).	☐	☐
• Difficulty tolerating interpersonal conflict, ambiguity, and uncertainty.	☐	☐
• May use avoidance and/or externalization in potentially challenging situation	☐	☐

Foundational Competencies: 3. Relationships

B. Consultation and Functioning in Interprofessional Systems	Mid	End
Advanced Skills/Performance:		
• Incorporates psychological information into overall team care planning and implementation.	☐	☐
• Effectively manages team dynamics including the complexities related to role overlap and conflict with other professionals.	☐	☐
• Uses skills as a psychologist to facilitate team functioning, taking leadership role appropriately, including providing consultation to team leaders regarding team functioning.	☐	☐
• Takes leadership role when appropriate and contributes to effective patient/client care by proactively sharing information with team.	☐	☐
High Intermediate Skills/Performance:		
• Independently contributes to interprofessional team, such as:		
• Proactively communicating important information about patients.	☐	☐
• Being sensitive to the dynamics of the team(s) on which the trainee is working and responding to the needs of other team members and appropriately.	☐	☐
• Identifying areas of role overlap and sources and types of conflict	☐	☐
• Occasional focus of supervision is to determine how best to communicate information or feedback or to process any challenging complex team issues.	☐	☐

Intermediate Skills/Performance:		
• Has developed an understanding of the interprofessional team and the role of all the professionals on the team including that of the psychologist.	☐	☐
• Supervision focus is on one or more of the following:		
• Providing to the treatment team relevant patient information concisely and/or at appropriate times.	☐	☐
• Applying his/her understanding of complex or challenging interactions between team members to improve patient /client care.	☐	☐
• Understanding role overlap related to the functioning of team members and the psychologist on this team.	☐	☐
Novice Skills/Performance:		
• Demonstrates ability to cooperate with others in task completion, but will often let others take lead even if knowledgeable about area.	☐	☐
• Supervision focuses on one or more of the following:		
• Participating appropriately in team discussions.	☐	☐
• Making relevant, well-stated contributions to case management of patients.	☐	☐
• Understands and demonstrates respect for the usual role and function of the psychologist and other team members and how this contributes to establishing and meeting patient goals	☐	☐
• Understands the principles of team functioning and how they affect patient/client care.	☐	☐
Does not Meet Expectations:		
• Despite supervision, has limited knowledge of and ability to display the skills that support effective interprofessional team functioning, such as:		
• Demonstrating respect for the unique skills of other team members.	☐	☐
• Understanding the importance of interprofessional communication/collaboration in optimizing patient care.	☐	☐

Functional Competencies: 1. Assessment And Treatment Planning

A. Psychological Assessment and Diagnostic Skills	Mid	End
Advanced Skills/Performance:		
• Independently selects assessment tools that reflect awareness of patient population served at practice site.	☐	☐
• Administers scores and interprets test results taking into account limitations of the evaluation method.	☐	☐
• Regularly and independently identifies/integrates pertinent clinical information that is related to the patients' context, incorporating cultural factors, and makes appropriate diagnosis	☐	☐
High Intermediate Skills/Performance:		
• Strong ability to select and administer psychological tests appropriate to referral questions and patient population.	☐	☐
• Supervision focus is on refining one or more of the following:	☐	☐
• Fine points of test administration and/or interpretation.	☐	☐
• Reassurance that selected tests are appropriate.		
• Complex cases, referral questions, and/or diagnostic conclusions.	☐	☐
Intermediate Skills/Performance:		
• Selects assessment tools that reflect awareness of patient population served at a given practice site.	☐	☐
• Demonstrates ability to adapt environment and materials according to client needs (e.g., lighting, privacy, ambient noise, medications, health condition, disability).	☐	☐
• Supervision focus is of refining one or more of the following:	☐	☐
• Determining appropriate tests for referral questions.	☐	☐
• Understanding the role of culture, developmental level, medical stability, and/or disability in test selection and interpretation.	☐	☐
• Administration and/or test scoring procedures.	☐	☐
• Interpreting unusual findings or novel tests.	☐	☐
• Integration of testing data and/or collateral information into diagnostic conclusions	☐	☐
Novice Skills/Performance:		
• Has basic knowledge regarding the assessment of a range of normative and clinical manifestations of issues in the context of human development and diversity.	☐	☐
• Supervision focus is skill development in one or more of the following area:	☐	☐
• Integrating all relevant patient data.	☐	☐
• Integrating collateral information (e.g., medical/education/ employment/developmental/legal records).	☐	☐
• Test selection, execution, and accuracy of conclusions.	☐	☐
• Considering alternative diagnoses/identifying rule out diagnoses	☐	☐
• Considering cultural or contextual factors.	☐	☐

Does not Meet Expectations:		
• Intensive supervision required, with measurable objectives, on (please specify):	☐	☐

Functional Competencies: 1. Assessment and Treatment Planning

B. Treatment Planning Skills	Mid	End
Advanced Skills/Performance:		
• Consistently establishes effective relationships with a wide variety of patients.	☐	☐
• Understands and uses own emotional reactions to the patient productively as part of treatment planning.	☐	☐
High Intermediate Skills/Performance:		
• Works collaboratively with patient and smoothly facilitates agreement about treatment goals.	☐	☐
• Sophisticated ability to develop a comprehensive treatment plan, including appropriate and realistic goals.	☐	☐
• Occasional supervision focuses on assessing patient response to treatment plan and determining how best to address barriers in order to maximize progress early in treatment.	☐	☐
Intermediate Skills/Performance:		
• Develops rapport with most clients.	☐	☐
• Participates actively in treatment planning using an evidence-based approach.	☐	☐
		☐
• Can identify own issues that may impact therapeutic process.	☐	☐
• Supervision focuses on one or more of the following:	☐	☐
• Determining how to respond to patient agenda as part of treatment planning process.	☐	☐
• Maintaining focus in treatment planning session.	☐	☐
Novice Skills/Performance:		
• Articulates awareness of theoretical/empirical basis for choosing treatment focus and approach.	☐	☐
• Supervision focuses on one or more of the following:	☐	☐
• Developing treatment plan and goals.	☐	☐
• Generating hypotheses/interpretations.	☐	☐
• Increasing ability to individualize treatment to individual patient.	☐	☐
• Identifying own emotional reactions to the patient.	☐	☐
Does not Meet Expectations:		
• Has difficulty developing rapport with most patients.	☐	☐
• Intensive supervision, with measurable objectives, is required to allow for maintenance of therapeutic alliance.	☐	☐

Functional Competencies: 2. Supervision

A. Participation in Supervision Process	Mid	End
Advanced Skills/Performance:		
• Proactively seeks consultation when complex or unfamiliar cases/situations arise and effectively integrates input/feedback.	☐	☐
• Anticipates and structures optimal use of supervision time.	☐	☐
• Uses supervision to refine and consolidate professional identity.	☐	☐
• Independently obtains information to enhance clinical practice and brings to supervision for discussion.	☐	☐
• Elucidates clear and appropriate professional training goals.	☐	☐
High Intermediate Skills/Performance:		
• Always open and responsive to feedback.	☐	☐
• Demonstrates knowledge of limits of competency (i.e., assesses metacompetency) to a degree that broad, close supervisory oversight is not needed.	☐	☐
	☐	☐
Intermediate Skills/Performance:		
• Routinely prepared for supervision with agenda of questions/ issues to discuss.	☐	☐
• Generally cognizant of strengths and areas for improvement and open to such discussion.	☐	☐
• Supervisor input clearly enhances skill set and general professional development.	☐	☐
• Demonstrates application of supervisor feedback in subsequent work.	☐	☐
• Supervision used to highlight avenues for continued learning.	☐	☐
Novice Skills/Performance:		
• Demonstrates basic knowledge of supervision models and practice.	☐	☐
• Is developing awareness and skills around optimal use of supervision time.	☐	☐
• Able to integrate feedback into self-assessment and demonstrates interpersonal skills of communication and openness to feedback.	☐	☐
• Emerging awareness of areas of strength and areas of growth.	☐	☐
Does not Meet Expectations:		
• Requires a significant amount of time in supervision, without a commensurate increase in knowledge/skills.	☐	☐
• Has difficulty engaging in professional reflection about his/her clinical relationships with supervisors.	☐	☐
• Is disrespectful of supervisor.	☐	☐

Functional Competencies: 2. Supervision

B. Professional Development: Efficiency and Prioritization	Mid	End
Advanced Skills/Performance:		
• Efficient and effective time management.	☐	☐
• Independently and accurately makes adjustments to priorities as demands evolve.	☐	☐
• Ensures that routine and nonroutine tasks are accomplished as required.	☐	☐
High Intermediate Skills/Performance:		
• Supervision may focus on minor suggestions regarding judgment of prioritization.	☐	☐
• Keeps supervisors aware of whereabouts as needed.	☐	☐
Intermediate Skills/Performance:		
• Completes work effectively and promptly by using supervision time for priority setting.	☐	☐
• Accomplishes tasks in a timely manner, but needs occasional deadlines or reminders.	☐	☐
• Identifies priorities but needs input to structure some aspects of task.	☐	☐
• Keeps scheduled appointments and meetings on time.	☐	☐
Novice Skills/Performance:		
• Needs some supervisory guidance to successfully accomplish large tasks within the timeframe allotted.	☐	☐
• At times, student takes on responsibility and has difficulty asking for guidance or accomplishing goals within timeframe.	☐	☐
• Regularly needs deadlines or reminders.	☐	☐
Does not Meet Expectations:		
• Frequent tardiness and/or unaccounted absences are a problem.	☐	☐
• Not receptive to supervisory input about difficulties.	☐	☐

About the Authors

Dr. Julie Gosselin, R.Psych is the Director of Clinical Training for the Psy.D. program and Associate Professor of Clinical Psychology at Memorial University of Newfoundland. She is also Adjunct Professor of Psychology at the University of Ottawa.

Dr. Mélanie Joanisse, C.Psych is a clinical and health psychologist who works at the Montfort Hospital, Clarence-Rockland Family Health Team, and The Ottawa Couple and Family Institute. She is a clinical professor at the University of Ottawa and associate professor at Université du Québec en Outaouais.

Index

Alliance, behaviors, cognition, dynamics, and existentials (ABCDE) model, 63–64
American Psychological Association (APA), 2
Anxious symptomatology, 103
Assessment competency development
  evaluating, 119
  training goals for, 116–119

Canadian Interprofessional Health Collaborative (CIHC), 24
Capacity and self-care, 69–71
Circle of care, 104
Client motivation, assessing, 105
Clinician-related variables
  clinical case vignette, 55–57
  psychological assessment, 40–41
Cognitive behavioural therapy (CBT), 4
  emotion-focused, 10
Competency-based evaluation, 119
Composite International Diagnostic Interview (CIDI), 33
Contextual variables
  clinical case vignette, 55–57
  psychological assessment, 40–41

Depressive/anxious episodes, 97
Differential referral model, 21
DSM-5, 3
Dysregulation, avoiding, 96

Ecosystemic approach, psychological assessment, 35–37
  case study for, 36
  chronosystem, 35–36
  clinical case vignette, 50–52
  exosystem, 35
  macrosystem, 35
  microsystem, 35
  ontosystem, 35
Emancipation, process of, 116

Emotion-focused CBT, 10
Empirically supported treatment (EST), 6–9
Evidence-based medicine model, 23
Evidence-based practice (EBP)
  and clinical competency development, 115
  clinician–patient relationship, 5
  definition of, 2–3
  diagnosis as case formulation, 4–5
  empirically supported treatment (EST), 6–9
  and integration, 9–11
  main issues of, 3
  to manualize evidence-based treatment plans, 5–6
  from medicine to psychology, 2–3
  misconceptions of, 3–9
  Presidential Task Force on, 2
Evidence-based practice in psychology (EBPP), 2
Evidence-based treatment (EBT), 5–6, 62

Functional competencies, 20

Goal specificity, 117

Improving Access to Psychological Therapies (IAPT) program, 8
Integrative assimilation, 22
Interdisciplinary collaboration
  clinical case vignette, 52–54
  psychological assessment, 37–39
Interprofessional collaboration
  competency domains for effective, 24
  definition of, 24
Interprofessional competencies, 24
Interprofessional model
  for psychological assessment, 31–41
  case formulation framework, 41–42, 57–59

clinical case vignette, 45–59
clinician-related and contextual
    variables, 40–41, 55–57
development of, 32
ecosystemic factors, 35–37,
    50–52
as general framework for
    professional practice, 31
interdisciplinary collaboration,
    37–39, 52–54
personal history, 34–35, 48–50
prognostic considerations, 39,
    54–55
symptoms, 33–34, 46–48
for psychological treatment
    planning, 64–82
accountable to clients, 66
dimensions included in, 68–69
evidence-based, 65
relational/attachment-based,
    64–65
strength-based, 65–66
treatment delivery and monitoring,
    85–93
clinical case vignette, 85–91
importance of, 112
treatment plan
creating, 73–82
client feedback about, 112
client response to, 111
collaborative agreement for, 112
planning session, 95–112
treatment spheres, 66–73, 107
capacity and self-care, 69–71,
    76–78
mastery and competence of self,
    71–72, 78–80
mastery and competence with
    others, 72–73, 80–82

Mastery and competence of self,
    71–72
Mastery and competence with others,
    72–73
Mini International Neuropsychiatric
    Interview (MINI), 33
Modern clinician

assessment and treatment planning
    model for, 19–27
competency-based approach, 19–20
development of competencies,
    25–26
differential referral model, 21
evidence-based approach, 25
functional competencies, 20
integrative approach, 21–22
interprofessional collaboration, 24
patient-centred approach, 25
prioritization, in treatment
    planning, 22
professional development,
    importance of, 19
professionalism, 26
reflective practice competency, 27
Multidimensional model, of human
    functioning, 63
Multitheoretical therapy
    framework, 63

National Interprofessional
    Competency Framework, 24

Potential contradictions, to
    treatment, 99
Presidential Task Force, on EBP, 2
Prioritization, in treatment
    planning, 22
Professionalism, 40
compassion, 26
definition of, 26
fiduciary relationship, 26
trust, 26
Prognostic considerations
clinical case vignette, 54–55
psychological
    assessment, 39
Proximal development, zone of,
    117–118
Psychological assessment
case formulation framework, 41–
    42, 57–59, 105
clinical case vignette, 45–59
clinician-related and contextual
    variables, 40–41, 55–57

competency in, development of,
    113–119
ecosystemic factors, 35–37,
    50–52, 101
interdisciplinary collaboration,
    37–39, 52–54
interprofessional model0 for,
    31–41
model for modern clinician, 19–27
personal history, 34–35, 48–50, 98
prognostic considerations, 39,
    54–55, 104
symptoms, 33–34, 46–48, 96
Psychological treatment planning and
    monitoring competency in,
    development of, 113–119
interprofessional model for, 64–82
    accountable to clients, 66
    dimensions included in, 68–69
    evidence-based, 65
    relational/attachment-based,
        64–65
    strength-based, 65–66
model for modern clinician, 19–27
other integrative models, 62–64
    ABCDE model, 63–64
    multidimensional model of
        human functioning,
        63–64
    multitheoretical therapy
        framework, 63
    transtheoretical model, 62
treatment delivery and monitoring,
    85–93
    clinical case vignette, 85–91
    importance of, 112
treatment plan, creating, 73–82
    client feedback about, 112
    client response to, 111
    collaborative agreement for, 112
treatment planning session, 95–112
treatment spheres, 66–73, 107
    capacity and self-care, 69–71,
        76–78
    clinical case vignette, 85–93
    mastery and competence of self,
        71–72, 78–80

mastery and competence with
    others, 72–73, 80–82
Psychology competency framework,
    115–116
Psychotherapy integration
    evidence-based practice (EBP)
        definition of, 2–3
    diagnosis as case formulation, 4–5
    empirically supported treatment
        (EST), 6–9
    and integration, 9–11
    to manualize evidence-based
        treatment plans, 5–6
    from medicine to psychology, 2–3
    misconceptions of, 3–9
    Presidential Task Force on, 2
    transtheoretical model for, 1–11

Randomized clinical trial (RCT), 3,
    6–7
Reflective practice competency, 27, 40

Self-criticism, ignoring, 98
Sense of safety, developing, 97
Social and emotional support, 102
Structured Clinical Interview for
    DSM-5 (SCID-5), 33
Suicidal risk, screening for, 99
Supervision
    administrative/evaluative role, 114
    counseling/supportive role, 114
    definition of, 113–114
    didactic/training role, 114
    feedback on regular basis, 119
    mentoring/professional
        development role, 114
    monitoring/consulting role, 114

Task Force on Promotion
        and Dissemination of
        Psychological Procedures, 7, 8
Technical eclecticism, 21
Transtheoretical model, 62
Treatment delivery and monitoring,
    85–93
    clinical case vignette, 85–91
    importance of, 112

Treatment plan
   creating, 73–82
   client feedback about, 112
   client response to, 111
   collaborative agreement
        for, 112
   planning session, 95–112

Treatment spheres, 66–73, 107
   capacity and self-care, 69–71,
        76–78
   mastery and competence of self,
        71–72, 78–80
   mastery and competence with
        others, 72–73, 80–82

OTHER FORTHCOMING TITLES FROM OUR DEVELOPING A COMPETENCY BASED MENTAL HEALTH PRACTICE COLLECTION

Julie Gosselin, *Editor*

Systems and Management in Clinical Psychology
by Andrea Piotrowski

How to Use and Conduct Clinical Supervision: A Supervisor-Supervisee Approach by Edward A. Johnson

Momentum Press is one of the leading book publishers in the field of engineering, mathematics, health, and applied sciences. Momentum Press offers over 30 collections, including Aerospace, Biomedical, Civil, Environmental, Nanomaterials, Geotechnical, and many others.

Momentum Press is actively seeking collection editors as well as authors. For more information about becoming an MP author or collection editor, please visit http://www.momentumpress.net/contact

Announcing Digital Content Crafted by Librarians

Momentum Press offers digital content as authoritative treatments of advanced engineering topics by leaders in their field. Hosted on ebrary, MP provides practitioners, researchers, faculty, and students in engineering, science, and industry with innovative electronic content in sensors and controls engineering, advanced energy engineering, manufacturing, and materials science.

Momentum Press offers library-friendly terms:

- perpetual access for a one-time fee
- no subscriptions or access fees required
- unlimited concurrent usage permitted
- downloadable PDFs provided
- free MARC records included
- free trials

The **Momentum Press** digital library is very affordable, with no obligation to buy in future years.

For more information, please visit **www.momentumpress.net/library** or to set up a trial in the US, please contact **mpsales@globalpress.com**.